Key Competencies for Whole-System Change

D0205205

LEADERSHIP

Lyle Kirtman

Michael Fullan

Solution Tree | Press

a division of
Solution Tree

555 North Morton Street
Bloomington, IN 47404
800.733.6786 (toll free) / 812.336.7700
FAX: 812.336.7790

email: info@solution-tree.com
solution-tree.com

Printed in the United States of America

19   18   17   16   4   5

Library of Congress Cataloging-in-Publication Data

Kirtman, Lyle.

    Leadership : key competencies for whole-system change / by Lyle Kirtman and Michael Fullan.

        pages cm

    Includes bibliographical references and index.

    ISBN 978-1-936763-52-8 (perfect bound) 1. Educational leadership--United States. 2. Educational change--United States. 3. School management and organization--United States. I. Fullan, Michael. II. Title.

    LB2805.K5235 2016

    371.2--dc23

                                            2015021614

Solution Tree
Jeffrey C. Jones, CEO
Edmund M. Ackerman, President

Solution Tree Press
President: Douglas M. Rife
Associate Acquisitions Editor: Kari Gillesse
Editorial Director: Lesley Bolton
Managing Production Editor: Caroline Weiss
Senior Production Editor: Suzanne Kraszewski
Copy Editor: Sarah Payne-Mills
Proofreader: Elisabeth Abrams
Text and Cover Designer: Rian Anderson
Compositor: Abigail Bowen

Acknowledgments

I would like to thank Claire Rickey (my mother) who always inspired me to be fearless in my leadership and not let convention hold me back; to my wife Kathy for her patience and support of my crazy hours; Stephan Kohler, a friend and a colleague who has always believed in me and challenged me to do my best work; Beth Saunders, a leadership partner in my work and the calmness I always need in the office, and a great editor, too; Bobbie D'Alessandro, a great leader who has always believed in my work; John Pierce, an amazing principal and coach who is always my thought partner; and Valerie Spriggs, an inspiring leader and coach to me.

— Lyle Kirtman

To my great team and colleagues who do fantastic work individually and together: Eleanor Adam, Claudia Cuttress, Mary Jean Gallagher, Andy Hargreaves, Bill Hogarth, Joanne McEachen, John Malloy, Joanne Quinn, Santiago Rincon-Gallardo, and Laura Schwalm, and to our many coconspirators in California, Canada, Australia, New Zealand, and more. Thank you all for generating insights and ideas for leading system change. I am grateful for all those times where friendship and professionalism meet.

— Michael Fullan

Solution Tree Press would like to thank the following reviewers:

John E. Ash
Principal
Central Magnet School
Murfreesboro, Tennessee

Nannette Johnston
Superintendent
Hardin County Schools
Elizabethtown, Kentucky

Henry Madsen
Principal
Ellerslie Campus
Edmonton, Alberta, Canada

Kimberly Moritz
Superintendent
Randolph Central School
    District
Randolph, New York

Tamara Rasmussen
Coach
Oregon Response to
    Intervention
Roseburg, Oregon

Henry B. Russell
Associate Professor
Educational Leadership and
    Human Development
University of Central Missouri
    Warrensburg, Missouri

Table of Contents

CHAPTER 7

Changing the Game—Anytime, Anywhere 107

CHAPTER 8

Creating System Breakthroughs—
You Are Needed 123

About the Authors

 Lyle **Kirtman** is a management con-
sultant with more than twenty-five
years of experience. He specializes in leadership and organizational development,
strategic planning, conflict resolution,
and executive coaching. He has consulted
with educational, nonprofit, corporate,
and government organizations, including
300 school districts, the Massachusetts
Municipal Association, and the U.S.
Environmental Protection Agency.

Lyle has served as chair of the Massachusetts governor's strategic
task force on innovation in education and as a senior manager for
Boston Public Schools. He is a frequent keynote speaker, webinar
and conference presenter, and radio and television guest.

Lyle earned a bachelor's degree in psychology from the State
University of New York (SUNY) and a master's degree in counsel-
ing with a concentration in career development from SUNY and
Fairfield University.

To learn more about Lyle's work, visit www.futuremsi.com and
follow him on Twitter @KirtmanLyle.

Michael Fullan is former dean of the Ontario Institute for Studies in Education at the University of Toronto. Recognized as an international authority on education reform, Michael is engaged in training, consulting, and evaluating change projects around the world. His ideas for managing change are used in many countries.

Michael led the evaluation team that conducted the assessment of the National Literacy and Numeracy Strategy in England from 1998 to 2003. Later, he was appointed special adviser to the premier and minister of education in Ontario.

In December 2012, Michael received the Order of Canada, one of Canada's highest civilian honors. The Order of Canada was established in 1967 to recognize a lifetime of outstanding achievement, dedication to community, and service to the nation.

Michael bases his work on the moral purpose of education as it is applied in schools and school systems to bring about major improvements. He has written several best-selling books that have been translated into many languages. His latest books include *The Principal: Three Keys for Maximizing Impact*, *Professional Capital* (with Andy Hargreaves), *Freedom to Change*, and *Coherence: The Right Drivers in Action for Schools, Districts, and Systems* (with Joanne Quinn).

To learn more about Michael's work, visit www.michaelfullan.ca and follow him on Twitter @MichaelFullan1.

To book Lyle Kirtman or Michael Fullan for professional development, contact pd@solution-tree.com.

Preface

As educational authors and researchers, we have been working independently for several decades but on the same pathways of improvement. Lyle's work has focused on the leadership competencies that educational leaders require as they encounter specific situations. Michael has examined leadership within the broader context of schools, districts, and state and national systems. Despite our different trajectories, we have both been advocates for changes in pedagogy that make a real difference in the learning experiences of students and educators and produced measurable results in learners' engagement and outcomes.

Everything we are involved in is grounded in *doing*. There is nothing distant, abstract, or theoretical about our work. The material in this book arises from the work we have done in partnership with many districts and states across the United States and Canada where we set out together to cause positive change—both in the big picture and at the school and community levels. The leadership we advocate is perfect for 21st century education, as it is made for conditions of uncertainty, which provide more elbow room, but also demand action. Success brings clarity and provides motivation to keep going. Whether leaders face uncertainty or have obtained clarity, they must always take initiative.

Leadership: Key Competencies for Whole-System Change examines how district and school leaders have turned the tide from a culture mired in countless independent initiatives and excessive compliance tasks to a culture in which leaders finally are saying, "Enough is enough!" These leaders believe that educational environments should be exciting, creative, and vibrant places for everyone involved. What's more, these leaders realize that *they do not have to wait for permission.* Far from being reprimanded for showing initiative, they instead gain professional and political power.

This book builds the case for expanding leadership at the local and regional levels with the support of leaders who realize there is a different way to do things. These local leaders spark system break-throughs and point the way to completely new and more effective ways to achieve widespread improvement on a deep level.

In chapter 1, we identify the problem of initiative overload and show how leaders can take action toward a more focused future. Chapter 2 lays out a set of core competencies—seven leadership competencies—that leaders need to simplify and better handle complex problems. Chapter 3 provides vignettes to illustrate each competency from leaders with whom we have worked. Chapter 4 outlines what leaders can do to clear the way for more effective action. Chapter 5 helps you set direction for creating innovative learning environments that are fun and productive. Chapter 6 examines how to increase productivity as new leaders will want to work in your organization. Chapter 7 shows that success can be achieved in any setting—rural, urban, and in between. The final chapter reveals the important idea that system breakthroughs come from the ground up.

This book gives leaders the tools to take action regardless of what level of the system they operate from. Indeed, our model is based on the premise that you have to be your own change agent and cause ripple effects by mastering the seven competencies as you lead change in your own jurisdiction and beyond.

Knowing You Are Not Alone

A s complicated as things are these days in education, the pressures we face as educators pave the path for a radical new way. Some of these pressures arise from the growing realization that the system is wracked with weaknesses; however, positive pressures join these negative pressures and inspire the creation of a new system. This is actually a very good time to be an educational leader, to identify kindred spirits, and to cultivate and mobilize real leaders. Despite this, many high-performing leaders feel alone.

High-performing leaders have forged a path to success that is against the grain and counter to the practices of their colleagues. They have felt the need to keep quiet about what they believe is needed to improve the education process. Such leaders feel they are destined to be alone because the majority of regulators and political leaders will be critical of their practices or, even worse, try to stop them. However, these pioneers are everywhere in the United States and around the world challenging the status quo in education but often feeling alone in their pursuit. In this book, we show that great leaders are really not alone; they have a network of colleagues who might be described as *below the radar*. Their greatness as leaders can be brought to the surface.

Surprisingly, these below-the-radar groups of leaders actually share common competencies, practices, and traits that make them successful. While they often do not have formal forums to convene and uncover their common practices, they share common ground, creating an extraordinary resource to their profession.

In fact, these great educational leaders share common ground with breakthrough leaders in industry, health care, and the public sector. In this book, we explore some examples from leaders in other professions to help improve the field of educational leadership.

Achieving Simplicity and Focus

Simple can be harder than complex: you have to work hard to get your thinking clear to make something simple. Steve Jobs, cofounder, chairman, and former CEO of Apple, believed that the key to making a difference in the world was through simplicity (Jobs, n.d.).

If our legislators and policy leaders understood the power and elegance of making life easier and simpler for educators, we could move mountains for our schools and districts and, ultimately, for our students.

We must move now to train and support leaders to simplify and focus their attention to fight off distractions. The teachers, principals, and administrators who commit their life work to students deserve an environment that is not mired in the complexity of red tape, regulations, and inane processes for the simplest of issues when all they ever wanted to do was look into a student's eyes, see her potential, and help her realize her dreams.

Educators in the 21st century often do not enjoy their work. They feel blamed for society's problems, and they spend too little time with students and other educators making the dream of education a reality. What has happened with education? Why did it get so cumbersome, complex, and unmanageable? Can we stop new mandates and regulations, or do we have to learn how to cope with this world of education in a new way?

We would like to say there is a simple answer. However, the bureaucracy that education has become has so many contributing factors it would take this whole book to address them. Politicians go in and out of office, each one adding his or her own mark to fixing education with new laws. The departments of education internationally, nationally, and in the states or provinces have their own ever-changing ideas about why education is not working and proposed solutions. Corporations, universities, and a myriad of educational change organizations also add their two cents about solving education's problems. We might even say that educational consultants like us often muddy the waters with our analyses.

We could try forever to unravel who or what is at the root of the problem in education and how to stop it. However, that would defeat the purpose of this book, which is to achieve simplicity and focus.

When we started our quest to help educators simplify and focus, we did so by compiling examples of successful education leaders we knew or had worked with. We were amazed at how many we could identify. Yes, the decades since *A Nation at Risk* was published (National Commission on Excellence in Education, 1983) have taken a toll on educators' energy, but at the same time, a growing number of leaders have had great success. It is these leaders—who have trumped the odds—who give us insight into how to achieve success, even under adverse circumstances. We can take advantage of this growing cadre of real leaders to identify insights and create new networks where good leaders working with other good leaders get even better.

This book tells the stories of how some district and school leaders have stopped the madness of the endless initiatives and mandates—the constant confusion and complexity—and simplified their world for the sake of their staff and students. It is hard work to focus your thinking amid the overload of demands. One must sort through complex, deep issues to make the world of education simple and powerful. We must think deeply about what our vision is for success and determine strategies and actions that we believe will move us to our goals and dreams for the future. Then, we must determine how we will know that our strategies are working and make quick course corrections to stay on track. This may sound complicated and cumbersome, but those who use the principles and strategies we identify in this book will find the way to make a difference.

Simplicity is the art and science of thinking, planning, and measuring our actions against the results we need to achieve. It is also about acting and learning as we go along. The best leaders commit to this reflection as a matter of course and relish the learning along the way. Mary Ann Jackman, former superintendent and a regional assistance director for the Massachusetts Department of Elementary and Secondary Education, states that to focus and simplify the work for underperforming districts, every school has to have a drumbeat. That drumbeat helps schools focus on and choose which initiatives and strategies will provide maximum impact for their desired results. She further explains that leaders should focus on three questions:

1. Is this the right initiative?

2. Is this the right time?

3. Is this the right intensity for implementation?

Mary Ann speaks of one high school that simplified and focused by examining its countless initiatives and decided to follow the drumbeat of vocabulary development and writing across the curriculum, which leveraged results for all subject areas (M. A. Jackman, personal communication, July 18, 2014).

Simplifying takes work, and it includes honoring the work of others and respecting the commitment they bring to the task. Maren Rocca Hunt, executive director of elementary education in Napa Valley Unified School District in California, notes that central office leaders must work as one unit—one cohesive team—and integrate their work to enable principals to do their best work for students (M. Rocca Hunt, personal communication, June 20, 2014).

This book provides our best thinking about how to make your life simple and meaningful as you meet the day-to-day challenges of educating students for our present and future world. A leader must simplify his or her work to allow the focus on results that everyone wants in his or her district or school. Once we decrease all the noise around us, we can focus our thinking and are thus less susceptible to the distractions that derail us from building great schools and districts. We believe that the road to success involves a combination of (1) using the right drivers for system success and (2) developing core competencies for continuous improvement.

Using the Right Drivers for System Success

The global stage of education has added to the complexity of education reform. The continuous pressure to turn around education is an obsession of policymakers. The United States, Australia, and a growing number of countries are trying to drive reform with better standards, assessments, monitoring, intervention, and teacher development. (By themselves, these are the *wrong policy drivers*, as we will address shortly.) Additionally, in some countries, such as the United States, the corporate community is pushing for results. Corporations are putting pressure on our education system to produce results and prepare students for the jobs of today and tomorrow.

By and large policymakers in the United States have misinterpreted the drive for results in the corporate world. There is a belief that improved education results can be achieved through accountability and compliance. In any successful business, the focus on results is about motivation and incentives, not compliance and accountability. Successful companies have simplified their systems to focus on customer needs and attracting and motivating the best staff. While all companies do have compliance and accountability functions, they are never touted as the key to success. They are designed to prevent problems—not produce results.

The wrong policy drivers have added layers of complexity and difficulty to education. Although the United States has used these strategies to drive initiatives, these requirements are not relevant in countries that have achieved admirable results in education or successful companies that have obtained results for their customers. This book will help you take a cue from these countries to dig through and remove the extra layers that have been added to education and have made your work more difficult.

While process is very important to sustain results, we must decrease the cumbersome processes for involving constituents in the work of schools and districts. Too often, leaders feel the need to set up numerous meetings with a variety of stakeholders. Without a clear plan, these meetings frequently lead to confusion and frustration as the link to action is unclear or nonexistent. While the input from people is important for results and credibility, the assumption that extra meetings will satisfy people who have concerns may not be true. We can, in many situations, gather input quickly and bring people along in supporting a change through the implementation process. Getting positive results is often more important to people than extra meetings that slow down progress. These processes slow down leaders' ability to get to the actions that generate results. What we refer to as *drivers* are policies and strategies that are intended to have a positive impact on performance. In examining whole-system change, which is central to any lasting solution in education, one of us, Fullan (2011) identifies four wrong drivers that have negative or neutral effects on performance, and four corresponding right drivers that make positive differences. The four wrong drivers are (1) negative accountability, (2) individualistic strategies, (3) technology, and (4) ad hoc policies. The right policy drivers—(1) capacity building, (2) teamwork, (3) pedagogy, and (4) systemic policies—when combined make a difference in system performance in regard to adult and student learning and achievement. Consider the following.

1. **Capacity building, not negative accountability:** A focus on accountability will stifle our ability to create cultures of excellence. We must move to capacity building.

2. **Teamwork, not individualistic strategies:** Group quality, not individual quality, allows the culture to use everyone's talents to obtain sustainable results. If you want to change the group, use the group for change.

3. **Pedagogy, not technology:** Technology is wonderful but only if it changes the way we think of instruction.

4. **Systemic policies, not ad hoc policies:** Fragmentation and constant discreet initiatives will never create sustainable results. The ability to think from a systemic viewpoint with integrated goals and strategies focuses the work of the education community.

Policymakers who are in a hurry to change the system and think they can legislate success use the wrong drivers. There is no evidence that these wrong drivers create sustainable change and improvement. In fact, the evidence is considerable that these policies have adverse effects on the system (Fullan, 2011).

Ironically, what looks like a quick route to success (the wrong drivers) actually slows down achievement. By contrast, the four right drivers work because they develop new capacities and cultures. To change the system, leaders must change the culture. Focusing on culture is a powerful way to establish a successful school district and system. Culture will always trump any initiative and determine whether a new program will work or not. Many educational policymakers think that a new curriculum and evaluation system will be the key to results. Yes, we need good curriculum standards and ways of assessing them, but we also need more effective pedagogy—how instructional practice can improve on a large scale. Developing pedagogy, or instructional practice, requires changes in school and district culture—the subject of the remaining chapters in this book.

Developing Core Competencies for Continuous Improvement

Our second organizing principle is that great leaders create the conditions for excellence and drive the cultural change needed to be successful. If we focus on the right drivers for cultural change and identify and support leaders who have the competencies to commit their work to these drivers, we will begin to see great schools and great districts globally. In fact, this book illustrates how many great leaders are already creating sustainable improvements. These great leaders can help you in your journey and can become part of your network for success. As Patrick Lencioni (2012) notes in his book *The Advantage,* a healthy organization is a place where leaders learn from one another, identify critical issues, and recover quickly from mistakes. He also lists five areas that are requirements for success and excellence.

1. Minimal politics

2. Minimal confusion

3. High morale

4. High productivity

5. Low turnover of talented leaders

We must use the right drivers to create the conditions for success and for preventing the formation of a culture that impedes excellence. This work begins with hiring the right leaders who have the competencies for creating healthy organizations that obtain sustainable results.

In this book we focus on seven core competencies originally developed by Lyle based on his research with over 600 leaders nationally and a subsequent study with 200 principals (Kirtman, 2014). In effect, the seven competencies integrate well with the four key right drivers: capacity building, teamwork, pedagogy, and systemic actions.

Moving Forward

You are not alone. Now is the time to reach forward, learn from, and connect with other leaders. The solution lies in achieving greater focus and in developing the core competencies that maximize implementation and continuous learning. In the next two chapters, we delve into the seven core leadership competencies. First, we name them and their subcomponents, and provide brief examples of what they look like in action. In chapter 3, we provide four vignettes that show the seven competencies combined in action.

Understanding the Seven Leadership Competencies

Consider the following: the health care industry used to focus on hospital reform. Then, the world of health care became complex, and the focus on individual hospitals as the vehicle for serving the complex needs of patients became limiting. Now, the health care world focuses on health care systems and networks of care. The same shift is imperative for education. Creating education networks and systems will break the paradigm of individuality that exists in education so that we can face challenges together and meet our goals, whether we are talking about districts with five schools or five hundred. Whether we are small or large, we must build partnerships with our community, state, nation, and even the world to serve students' multiple needs and prepare them for the global economy.

While this shift seems complicated, it can become simple if we hire the right leaders to create and maintain our education systems. These leaders must be able to direct the attention of the district toward sustainable improvement, which involves both managing distractions and setting clear organizational direction. Daniel Goleman (2013) defines attention as focusing on yourself, focusing on others, and focusing on the wider world. He further states that you need all three to be successful. Every leader needs to cultivate this triad of awareness, in abundance and in the proper balance, because a failure to focus inward leaves you rudderless, a failure to focus on others renders you clueless, and a failure to focus outward may leave you blindsided.

Kirtman's (2014) seven competencies (referred to in the previous chapter) are based on his data from several leadership self-assessments (DiSC, Myers-Briggs, and Workplace Personality Inventory [WPI]) and his observations of leaders in action for over thirty years. The seven competencies delineate the traits, characteristics, values, and behaviors of leaders who can focus on their own improvement, build capacity in others, and focus outwardly on the future trends in education. The seven competencies are as follows.

1. Challenges the status quo

2. Builds trust through clear communication and expectations

3. Creates a commonly owned plan for success

4. Focuses on team over self

5. Has a high sense of urgency for change and sustainable results in improving student achievement

6. Has a commitment to continuous improvement for self and organization

7. Builds external networks and partnerships

Figure 2.1 outlines the traits of each competency.

1.	**Challenges the Status Quo**
	a. Delegates compliance tasks to other staff
	b. Challenges common practices and traditions if they are blocking improvements
	c. Is willing to take risks
	d. Looks for innovations to get results
	e. Does not let rules and regulations block results and slow down action
2.	**Builds Trust Through Clear Communication and Expectations**
	a. Is direct and honest about performance expectations
	b. Follows through with actions on all commitments
	c. Makes sure there is a clear understanding based on written and verbal communication
	d. Is comfortable dealing with conflict
3.	**Creates a Commonly Owned Plan for Success**
	a. Creates written plans with input of stakeholders
	b. Ensures that people buy into the plan
	c. Monitors implementation of the plan
	d. Adjusts the plan based on new data and communicates changes clearly
	e. Develops clear measurement for each goal in the plan
	f. Creates short- and long-term plans

continued →

Figure 2.1: Kirtman's seven competencies for school leadership.

4.	**Focuses on Team Over Self**
	a. Hires the best people for the team
	b. Commits to the ongoing development of a high-performance leadership team
	c. Builds a team environment
	d. Seeks critical feedback
	e. Empowers staff to make decisions and get results
	f. Supports the professional development of all staff
5.	**Has a High Sense of Urgency for Change and Sustainable Results in Improving Student Achievement**
	a. Is able to move initiatives ahead quickly
	b. Can be very decisive
	c. Uses instructional data to support needed change
	d. Builds systemic strategies to ensure sustainability of change
	e. Sets a clear direction for the organization
	f. Is able to deal with and manage change effectively
6.	**Has a Commitment to Continuous Improvement for Self and Organization**
	a. Has a high sense of curiosity for new ways to get results
	b. Changes current practices for himself or herself and others willingly
	c. Listens to all team members to change practices to obtain results
	d. Takes responsibility for his or her own actions—no excuses
	e. Uses strong self-management and self-reflection skills

7.	**Builds External Networks and Partnerships**
	a. Sees his or her role as a leader in a broad manner that extends outside the work environment and community walls
	b. Understands his or her role as being a part of a variety of external networks for change and improvement
	c. Has a strong ability to engage people inside and outside the school setting in two-way partnerships
	d. Uses technology to expand and manage a network of resource people

Although the seven competencies are numbered, leaders' development of them and their application is *not* a linear process. There are circumstances that require the simultaneous application of more than one competency. There are other situations that warrant certain competencies move up to the forefront to obtain desired results.

For example, challenging the status quo is the first competency. This is intentional to emphasize that districts need to find effective methods to make the change process faster. Students' needs in the 21st century global society demand greater urgency of response. Too often the change process is too slow and gets mired in excessive process in an attempt to make all constituencies comfortable and supportive of the change. This does not mean that the new leader would challenge the existing culture the first week on the job, which would be a fast boot out the door. A new leader does need to enter his or her new culture and listen and learn rather than drive change immediately. However, challenging the status quo needs to be integrated into any entry process.

Building and sustaining success is not a linear process. The ability to know when to push and pull is key to all leaders' success. Knowing how to read the tea leaves when moving change forward and pulling back to ensure key people are on board are skills leaders can develop. Effective leaders focus on their audience. They have the ability to know when they have challenged people to begin to think differently about a problem but know when they need to pull back and let people think and own the change. This is a behavior we often see in great leaders. This is why the team aspect is so important. Every leader needs a team of leaders who can be open and honest in their feedback on when to push and when to pull. The additional perspective that a strong leadership team can provide to a principal can be extremely helpful. For example, additional information concerning which teachers need more of a push on challenging their assumptions about student learning or when it is time to pull back when the faculty is feeling overly criticized is invaluable to a principal. Each team member brings different skills and perspectives that, if used well, can provide a leader the intelligence to make the right decisions and effectively move forward to results for student achievement. Matt Geary, superintendent of the Manchester School District (Connecticut), is a master at reading the tea leaves. He is very clear about the urgency of results for students now but through his commitment to leadership development for his administrators is always taking the temperature of how people are managing the change process. He might not pull back for long, but he does realize that it takes time for people to integrate change into their practice (M. Geary, personal communication, September 12, 2014).

Now, we will explore each competency in detail.

Competency One: Challenges the Status Quo

In assessing leaders' competencies, Lyle (Kirtman, 2014) found that most leaders were highly compliant to state, federal, and local mandates and practices. Interestingly, this was *not* the case for the most effective leaders. High-performing leaders were not rule followers and not overly compliant. This did not mean that high-performing leaders broke any laws. It does mean, however, that the best leaders focus on results first and put less personal effort into ensuring that rules and compliance tasks are followed. They usually delegate the more transactional compliance tasks to others and have good systems to make sure the compliance work is completed. One way of describing it is that they are prepared to get a grade of C on compliance as long as they get an A on learning. Their priorities are to spend more time on developing other leaders and the group, creating a compelling vision for the school, and enhancing parent involvement than on completing compliance tasks.

Challenging common practices and traditions that block progress is also part of this competency. A leader must be able to respect traditions and community norms but also challenge their validity in a 21st century environment. If the norms are having a negative impact on student achievement results, leaders must challenge them respectfully.

Risk taking is another aspect of the first competency. Everyone has a different risk tolerance. We do not want to take risks with students' safety. However, trying a new practice for discipline that may engage a student in learning may be more effective than enforcing a rule or punishment. It is important that leaders keep student learning in the forefront of their minds at all times. The most effective leaders do not ask for permission, although they communicate often with their supervisor about their intended plans and seek counsel on how to be successful. This provides an opportunity for the supervisor to slow them down or help them change direction if necessary. This also allows leaders to keep moving if their supervisor does not engage in the issue in a timely manner. The trust that can build through this healthy partnership allows leaders to feel free to move ahead with their vision.

Being innovative is also part of challenging the status quo. Too often people say, "We have tried that approach before, and it did not work." Others might say that the innovation will create confusion and upset people. Innovation is a key to results for districts. We must try new approaches to reaching our students, gaining community support, and engaging our staff. Yes, innovation may not always be received positively in more conservative cultures. However, if traditions are valued and innovation is thoughtfully introduced, the results can be extraordinary.

Leaders must have the courage to challenge a district's or school's assumptions and traditions. Most school systems state that they want to prepare students for the 21st century, but they do not take the corresponding actions to test and make these changes. They often play it safe and avoid upsetting people, or worse, they end up hiring a high-profile leader who tries to blow up the status quo and create top-down change. In such cases, the message to a new leader coming in to the underperforming system is to get results now, while the system's culture is defensive and seems to take the stance of let's see who leaves first. The fear of change or job loss creates an antagonistic culture clash between change and preservation that usually results in the leader leaving in a short time with the battle scars remaining throughout the district. The leader may have achieved some short-term results, but he or she has not changed the culture to enable long-term success. Then, the school board or the superintendent hires a new leader to ease tensions and calm the waters. Change now takes a backseat, and the status quo prevails.

We will show how leaders have challenged the status quo and norms of the system and community to allow them to lead without fear. This, of course, means removing the shackles of accountability that the federal and state government use to restrict leaders from creating exciting cultures of innovation. The special skill set to challenge norms and gain support from the same people who feel they are charged with protecting and preserving those norms is essential for cultural change.

For example, one high-performing principal, Cate Cullinane, challenged her district's protocol for suspension. This middle school principal went against convention and showed courage and commitment by not suspending students for an early offense that she believed was not minor. She thought it was time to stop suspending students over and over again. She believed her work was not to suspend students but rather create a learning environment to engage students in self-management behavior. She also knew she needed parents to be her partners in this work on self-management.

When a student had a behavior issue, she met with the parents, explaining her goal and commitment to the teaching and learning process. Instead of suspending the student, she requested the parent work closely with her on educating and disciplining his or her child. The result was a dramatic decrease in suspensions in her school, while other principals continued to have increases. Additionally, the test scores went up, including the students who would have been suspended. Cate's experience showed that the vast majority of parents appreciate being informed that their child's behavior is disruptive to his or her education or steals the education of others in the class. She found that a phone call to a parent after the third time a child had been asked to leave the class prompted the parent to ask, "Why was I not called about this the first time?" Word spread quickly to students that parents will be called immediately when a problem occurs. Cate also spends time with students and parents on their goals for the future, which becomes motivating for the joint focus on education and decreases the negative behavior (C. Cullinane, personal communication, April 15, 2015).

Competency Two: Builds Trust Through Clear Communication and Expectations

Trust is a core factor in cultural change. Trust, of course, has to be earned—it can't just be obtained by leaders who say, "Please trust me." Our rule of thumb for developing trust is to "name it, model it, and monitor it." Trust is also enhanced when the leader builds a talented effective team. In his research, Lyle (Kirtman, 2014) defines *trust* in two ways. First, some leaders define it as whether they can count on a person to fulfill his or her commitments. Thus, reliability and efficacy are key indicators. The other definition that many leaders use is whether they can trust the person to not betray them or speak behind their back and do harm to their reputation.

As leaders, sometimes we can get lost in trying to establish trust with many groups that we have little time to work on our goals. In other words, trust and action go hand in hand. Kirtman (2014) found that effective leaders score high on a "sense of urgency for change." If a leader is clear in what she is saying and consistent in her actions, trust seems to thrive.

Another key area for trust building relates to clarity of performance expectations for staff *before* actions are required. If a leader is direct with his staff about what he expects from them to be successful, the trust seems to build and sustain over time. Trust is also built by fulfilling commitments and meeting deadlines. If a leader follows through, his staff can count on him, which ultimately builds trust.

Written and verbal communication directly affects trust. If one's spoken or written words are inconsistent or vague, mistrust can develop. For example, email is designed to enhance communication, but it can often be unclear and can create mistrust. Person-to-person communication is often critical to building trust with email used as follow-up for documentation and deadlines.

Finally, a leader's ability to deal with conflict is very important to building trust. If a leader avoids conflict or hopes it will get better on its own, the conflict can erode trust. If the leader deals with conflict head on, he or she can rectify the situation before it affects trust. In fact, if handled well, conflict can increase trust.

Following is an example of how communicating and setting clear expectations can simplify the complex concept of trust. Lyle acted as a coach for a suburban district principal who was a very caring and sensitive man. He believed in his faculty and cared deeply for students. His school was mired in mediocrity. When asked what one change or intervention he believed would start edging his school to excellence, he responded immediately about how he supported teachers. As a coach, Lyle was supportive, but in a direct manner he asked, "Support is fine, but is it leading to improved student achievement?" The principal struggled with the question. He was stuck in the inertia of passive support—not willing or able to take action that would simultaneously challenge the status quo and provide teachers with more demanding and clearer expectations and associated actions.

This principal was reticent to give his opinion because he was afraid that his teachers would be upset. Eventually, the principal, with confidence, said that increasing student engagement would be a key factor for success. He was then asked about how he would tell his faculty that he believed student engagement was critical for success. The principal fell back to his previous approach and stated that over the year he would have conversations with faculty and try to find opportunities to coach staff on increasing their engagement with students. Lyle responded again with clarity and passion. Using the competency of building trust through clear communication and expectations, he challenged the principal to decrease his fear of losing relationships and to start the year by presenting in his opening speech the importance of increasing student engagement.

The principal took Lyle's coaching advice and started the school year with a clear expectation that teachers would engage students. His worry that the faculty would be upset turned out to be completely unwarranted. The principal used his strength of being supportive and caring to convey that he would help each faculty member improve his or her skills in student engagement.

The school collectively focused on his clear expectation, and test scores subsequently increased. It is not always this straightforward, but here we have a leader, with assistance from a persistent coach, who took the chance of challenging the status quo and developing trust and supporting high expectations. A reticent principal, whose teachers actually wanted to move in this direction, was rewarded when he took the chance to act in a focused manner.

Competency Three: Creates a Commonly Owned Plan for Success

Leaders who can analyze complex data and situations and think, plan, and act systemically are successful in education. As state and federal initiatives and directives add new plans every year and fragment our schools and districts, leaders who are successful in simplifying and consolidating their plans are better able to advance their goals.

One of the key lessons from Michael's *motion leadership* work (leadership that moves individuals and leaders forward) is "beware of fat plans" (Fullan, 2010, p. 24). There seems to be a tendency on the part of leaders to create great-looking, comprehensive plans that end up on a shelf. Better to develop short plans (two or three pages) that are inspiring, "sticky," action oriented, and alive for implementers. Skinny, focused plans are *sticky* because they are close and connected to day-to-day actions. One guideline for leaders is to remember that ultimately implementation plans are for the implementers, not the planners.

We will show how successful leaders have taken multiple complex plans for technology, parent involvement, student achievement, accreditation, special education, and many more areas and created one- to two-page plans for success. Though short, these plans can meet all the requirements and mandates to map the road to success.

Fragmentation from overly complex plans creates extra, unnecessary work that ties up the same people in attending countless meetings and drafting and editing endless documents to implement high-leverage goals and strategies for success. People do need to have something in writing to look at and refer to as they navigate the waters of constant change. The plan needs to be clear and easy to update as conditions change. We must be able to easily monitor success to determine the need for course corrections. If the measurements are too cumbersome to allow for quick assessment, the change will be too little and too late to make a difference. Later, we review the process of strategic planning and identify the aspects that allow for fast results—simple, skinny planning documents are more effective than elaborate ones that look great on paper but do not work in reality. Often the time and effort of a strategic plan exhaust a school and system, preventing educators from learning from implementation. It is important to shorten the process up front and lengthen the interactive effort of learning from implementation.

Technology can be a key driver in strategic planning. However, when treated as a separate initiative, technology loses its impact for change through a lack of integration into the teaching and learning process, thus being a negative driver; however, when pedagogy is linked to results, technology can accelerate learning. In Fullan's (2013) book *Stratosphere,* he shows that the typical approach to adding technology is to purchase it without much thought given to how it will be used to further learning. In his follow-up work on new pedagogies for deep learning, he provides several examples with respect to how pedagogy becomes the foundation for which technology is the accelerator for deep learning (see especially the video on Park Manor at www.michaelfullan.ca).

One principal in an urban environment with a large population of at-risk students was heading into a school year on a state-improvement plan. In addition, each district initiative required a plan and a technology plan. The stack of plans was almost ten inches high when put on a table. No one could speak about what was in the plans because they were so unmanageable.

With the help of a coach, the principal learned about the benefits of adopting the one- to two-page skinny plan approach to decrease the paper and develop a laser focus for improving student achievement. The team then developed a two-page plan complete with the principal's clear expectations. In many states, the focus on improvement is directed at a complicated evaluation process for performance of teachers and administrators. As Fullan (2014) shows, such procedures lead principals down a path of micromanagement that is as ineffective as it is unwanted by teachers and principals alike. These monitoring documents are often hundreds of pages with more than thirty rubrics for improvement. If an administrator tried to implement these plans as stated, he or she would have little time to ever meet with teachers and coach them for improved instruction.

The streamlined approach became the subject of continual discussions with faculty, the central office, and the community. Each key meeting involved updating the plan, celebrating successes, and refocusing priorities that were beginning to drift.

The school is no longer designated as underperforming, and the district is adopting its planning process. Now, school staff can tell you what the plan says and what it means to them in terms of their role and contributions. Skinny plans include:

1. A clear vision, mission, context, or description of what problem needs to be solved

2. High-level strategies and initiatives for major impact on student achievement

3. Reference to other plans that might be required by the state or federal government

4. Key timelines for high-level action

Competency Four: Focuses on Team Over Self

This competency connects strongly to two drivers for system success: (1) capacity building and (2) teamwork. Thus, this team-building competency is a high-leverage aspect of cultural change.

Ultimately, a leader is only successful if he has built leadership capacity in his school and district. A team is a group of leaders with a common purpose and set of goals who work to implement them to completion and to achieve results. According to Jon Katzenbach and Douglas Smith (1993), "A team is a small number of people with complementary skills who are committed to a common purpose, set of performance goals, and approach for which they hold themselves mutually accountable" (p. 111).

Unfortunately, many leaders do not realize that they cannot just put a group of people together and call it a team. It takes hard work to build a highly effective team that helps the leader build a results-oriented culture. In addition, leaders must be able to self-reflect and become voracious learners about their own strengths and areas for growth. A leader's vulnerability and openness for honest feedback are crucial for true team development and capacity building. We review tools and practices necessary for leaders to sustain their learning journey using real-life examples and reflections.

A high-performing leader hires the best people and never settles for second best. Many leaders panic and put warm bodies in key roles when no great candidates have emerged. These leaders always look back and say, "I wish I did not settle," because a poor performer drags down a team's results and is hard to remove. It is better to keep looking for the best person and fill the position on an interim basis.

Teams are not static. Every time a new person joins, the team dynamics change. The best teams constantly work on their development and improvement. A leader must be secure in his or her confidence and ability to lead and be willing to hear critical feedback and support the team even if he or she would do things differently. The leader needs to focus on outcomes and results—not on how the work is done. Empowering people to work together and seek guidance from one another will achieve better results than top-down leadership.

Often leaders claim they know what their teammates think of them and how they are perceived. We have found that most leaders are wrong about their perception and underestimate the subtleties that exist in forming teams that can derail success. In this book, you will hear about leaders who have strong moral imperatives and self-awareness that guide them every day and allow them to stay steady when they feel attacked or when their self-confidence begins to erode. Laura Schwalm, former superintendent of Garden Grove School District in Anaheim, California, who we will meet later, represents a superb example of having a strong moral compass that she combines with an equally strong action bend to fulfill the district's mission.

A leader needs to distribute the leadership, not just delegate tasks. For example, a principal can ask his or her assistant principal to lead the implementation of a goal on improving morale. A superintendent might delegate to a staff member the researching of what private schools in the community offer that may be competing with the district. If a leader builds a team that is truly effective, the team can function whether or not the principal is in the school. The leader can then focus on providing professional development to the team and to each individual staff member to improve his or her leadership skills.

The following story about a Midwestern superintendent in the months before 9/11 demonstrates the power of a team. The district had a management team (not a true leadership team). Each school and department reported on its work at management team meetings. The team received assignments and had very little collaboration unless the superintendent required it. The superintendent wanted to change this dynamic and create an interdependent team that acted from a system perspective, rather than a passive, silo-based perspective.

The superintendent began by establishing a new leadership team for the district. This change in nomenclature was only step one. Team members learned to examine themselves as leaders and to be direct and honest with each other for the betterment of the system. They learned to work together to help each member be successful. The superintendent began the process by being vulnerable and discussing his strengths and weaknesses and modeling a process of using leadership assessments to open up the discussion for each team member. The members of the team became more forthcoming in talking about their areas of strength and improvement based on leadership assessments and past evaluations.

On September 11, 2001, the superintendent was three hours away from the district. He immediately drove to the district to begin meeting with his team and planning a strategy for dealing with all the complexities it would face that day. When he arrived, he was shocked. The team members had all come together and met immediately after 9 a.m. and proceeded to develop a plan of action. They were well into the implementation of their plan when he walked in. No one waited; the team knew what it had to do and never hesitated. The superintendent was apprised of the plan, and he joined the team's effort. Sometimes you don't know the impact you are having until you see it in action.

Competency Five: Has a High Sense of Urgency for Change and Sustainable Results in Improving Student Achievement

Leaders who think systemically are often courageous and know how to create a results-oriented environment. Such leaders possess a sense of urgency for student results. This urgency is not reactive and crisis oriented; rather, it is strategic and purposeful to prepare students to be successful in their work and life. In education, adults often have trouble with fast change, but urgency is important. The world is changing so fast for our students. Education should not slow down change but rather enrich the change process.

Urgency means moving key initiatives forward quickly without too much process. Too many initiatives can overwhelm staff and create confusion and withdrawal. However, if the initiative is strategic, well thought out, and guided by the seven competencies in action, it can move ahead quickly.

Leaders practicing the fifth competency must be decisive. A leader who is too consensus oriented tries to please everyone, and the process can paralyze him or her. A strong leader can be decisive and move ahead quickly but adjust his or her strategies based on new data if the desired results are not reached. Moreover, the leader who has established a culture around the seven competencies will find that staff have also developed a strong sense of urgency for making progress.

The use of instructional data is critical to establishing a sense of urgency. However, sustainable change comes from creating a team-oriented learning environment where data are analyzed and used to determine needed change. If data are used to confront people on their poor or ineffective practice, it can create a blaming culture that will not result in sustainable change. If staff feel defensive, they will withdraw and miss opportunities to learn and change to meet student needs. Therefore, data must be used carefully to indicate areas for improvement, but must be delivered in a way that is motivating for change, not punitive and critical.

Change must be systemic. Change in one classroom or one school does not usually result in cohesive strategies for system change. If a new program is funded by a grant for a short period without developing a continual source of support, the program will die from lack of funding. Many districts have lost high-impact programs because of a lack of sustainable funding.

Too often, leaders successfully create a sense of urgency but do not know how to lead and manage the change process. The art and science of managing change is critical for leaders. Change is not a one-size-fits-all process. Leaders must also understand and support staff members' personal transitions. Each person deals with change individually. The new change could represent a loss of past practice to one person while another person sees the change as a welcomed opportunity.

For example, one high school principal was new to a relatively high-performing school where the faculty did not have a contract and were constantly in conflict and fighting each new innovation meant to prepare students for the 21st century. The school had no plan for change. Why did they need to change, staff wondered, when they were already among the best?

The leadership team was asked what it planned to do to move the school ahead and create a new culture of excellence and teamwork. The team responded that it would study the culture for the year and write a report to determine the approach for the next school year.

Instead, Lyle, the consultant, charged with helping the team create a sense of urgency, asked team members to decrease the process to one hour—perhaps a bit of an overstatement for dramatic effect. The principal and team were shocked. They worried that they were being fired and that the superintendent hired the consultant to drive them out. The consultant assured them that he was not there to fire them but to support them in their change initiatives. He pointed out that their long timeline and process would actually decrease their chance of success.

He believed this team could be successful and that its commitment to its students and families was admirable. He provided his assessment of the culture, pointing out the pervasive lack of leadership to achieve results and that team members were the ones who needed to turn the culture around. They listened intently and agreed with the assessment, acknowledging that they wanted to lead the change but needed support and help. The consultant, excited about the team's remarkable lack of defensiveness and admirable commitment to results, said he would be there to help.

The plan for action began. The team met twice a week, even during vacation for one month. The team then met with Lyle and the principal to review their work. The team proposed a restructuring of the leadership positions for the school. They created a position of academic affairs to gain focus on student achievement and determined that this may require hiring a new person. They were also focused on a new structure for discipline and realized that this would require a separate planning effort for the team. The discipline in the school was divided between three people and lacked a coherent strategy. They believed the new structure would allow the team to move initiatives forward faster. They realized that they needed to change more quickly rather than study the issues of discipline over the year, which was creating a reactive environment. The instructional data showed that while the school was successful, there were pockets of low performance and a schoolwide focus on instruction would improve all students' performance. The change needed to be comprehensive and not just focus on the source of stress or discipline. The new structure would set a new direction for the school of one school, not three houses. The team also realized that change is difficult and they would have to let go of the students they felt ownership for in their house. Instead, they had to think schoolwide and help all students achieve.

Sustainable change is an ongoing process and involves many more people in administration, the central office, and within the faculty. In fact, parents and community members, and finally the students themselves, need to be part of the new culture's design. Additionally, the change process can be remarkably faster than we think, *if* leaders exhibit the seven competencies. We will return to this key point later on.

Competency Six: Has a Commitment to Continuous Improvement for Self and Organization

The focus of the states and federal government on compliance, evaluation, and negative accountability creates cultures of caution and fear. Successful leaders embrace learning and improvement for themselves and their staff. When we are committed to continuous learning, we see that 21st century evaluation systems are cumbersome, punitive, restrictive, and limiting. More is accomplished in continuous learning environments than in environments based on fear and failure.

If a leader understands that the journey to great leadership is constant and never fully obtained, he or she tends to be a high performer. The principal who feels she has learned to be a great leader from her education or experience and does not continue the learning process often slips back to lower performance. Great leaders must be curious about what they can learn from others to always get better at their craft. They must be open to change even if they have been successful in the past with tried-and-true practices. Building an environment of continuous improvement requires a lot of listening. Extroverts are often excellent communicators and successful in reaching a range of constituents about their message and vision. However, if one talks too much or otherwise dominates and does not listen and really hear what others are saying or thinking, he or she will miss opportunities to learn as well as fail to develop key leaders in the school or district.

Leaders who are always striving to improve take responsibility for their actions and do not use excuses for mistakes or lack of results. If a leader believes that an excuse will relieve him of responsibility for results, he has taken the first step to failure. There are a range of challenges and barriers that great leaders face that can derail anyone. However, the best leaders find new ways to get results and never let any problem derail their success.

Finally, the high-performing, continuously improving leader is very strong at self-management. This leader does not triple-book meetings, arrive late to appointments, miss deadlines, or make promises she cannot meet. These leaders are always improving their skills in tracking projects, setting priorities, and getting results and are often ahead of deadlines. These leaders may need to have a strong assistant or team to support them on self-management, but they never abdicate personal responsibility to others.

Modern industries want students who are open to learning and experimenting and not fearful of failure. Despite this, in schools, we create evaluation systems based on a culture of fear. If we have leaders who are cautious and reticent to embrace the fast-changing world, then staff will face the same anxiety. Great leaders who embrace continuous learning still implement the required evaluation systems; however, they transform evaluation from a rating process that supports fear of failure to a goal-setting endeavor with dialogue that creates innovative processes for growth and development.

When an urban district bought into the concept of continuous improvement, staff were faced with changing demographics and the dramatic increase of at-risk populations. They were quite innovative but lacked focus and clarity. The number of administrators decreased in the district as resources diminished, and the leadership team felt overwhelmed and exhausted. Sound familiar? The district had a traditional evaluation process that was very compliant and not motivating to faculty and administrators. They struggled with providing direct feedback to people due to a previous culture of interest-based bargaining and collaboration. They had created a culture where direct feedback on performance was considered uncaring and insensitive and damaging to relationships.

Led by the superintendent and some of his key administrators, the district set out to change the culture to one of continuous improvement. Each administrator examined him- or herself as a leader and reflected on how he or she could improve. Administrators were then trained and coached to provide direct feedback to each other and to be honest about problems and concerns. No more behind-the-scenes conversations about problems!

They overcame their fear that honesty would damage their collaborative culture. The district's culture is now becoming much more direct and honest, and its previous commitment to collaboration has not only survived but flourished. Schools' innovations are now more focused, and they're addressing problems inhibiting results with a sense of urgency. Previous meetings were positive on the surface, but there was an undercurrent of frustration and a lack of focus. Meetings have now become places where continuous improvement and honesty rule.

Competency Seven: Builds External Networks and Partnerships

This final competency involves reaching out to form partnerships, access new ideas, and jointly solve problems with others. In this book, our best leaders will show how they find time to build their own networks of support. Technology and social networking can empower us, but too many educators fear them as vehicles for conflict and blame. A leader's ability to see the world as his or her network of support is a defining competency for today and in the future. You will hear how educators who are great leaders create true, expansive learning networks.

Partnerships that are a two-way street, built on a foundation of mutual respect, and focused on addressing specific problems create a push-and-pull dynamic that produces results. A principal is not just the school's leader; he or she is also a part of a district group of principals and the network of principals in the state, country, and world. Forming networks of colleagues and contacts in education and other fields is a key to success for great leaders.

A leader must know how to give and receive help from colleagues to feed and grow a support network. The days of only engaging people who can help you have long passed. We must be willing and able to help others fully develop two-way partnerships. To help people in our network, we must understand others' goals and needs and their organizations in order to help them meet their goals. This two-way relationship creates sustainable support, not just one-time assistance with a problem.

We must be able to get out of our office, school, district, and state or province to learn from others we might not think can offer us anything relevant for our work. You will be surprised to find out that the opportunities and resources are unlimited.

Most educators feel they have no time or do not know how to build networks and expand their leadership to building education systems. In this book, you will learn how to increase your resources by partnering with colleges, universities, community groups, private-sector businesses, and professionals. You will also learn how to help your partners achieve success instead of just asking them to help you. If leaders know how to build other leaders' networks, they will reap more benefits for their districts, schools, and students.

One superintendent in the southeast United States lived and breathed partnerships and created broad networks in her office and through the district. She built a culture of excellence and customer service that could be a model for any district. She never started a sentence on a new collaboration externally with the public or private sector with the word *no*. This superintendent was focused and strategic about how the partnerships would fit into her plans for improving student achievement. Therefore, the intensity and timing of the external relations ebbed and flowed based on needs and resources. The community faced dramatic financial cuts based on the politics of its state. This superintendent didn't let any problem stop her plan. She took a step back when the impact came but then immediately mobilized her support network. She went to her partners and asked them to help keep the district afloat. The community responded with support for the district. She did not have to cut one teacher or stop any key initiative that was critical to its desired results. Then, in a year, resources improved, and she could keep her base network and add new resources to enhance the district's strategies for success.

Seven Dynamic, Interactive Competencies

In this chapter, we have framed the leader's work in relation to the seven competencies derived from Lyle's study (Kirtman, 2014) of highly effective leaders. We have also provided brief examples from leaders with whom we have worked. Before proceeding to direct advice for leaders in chapters 4 and onward, we want to reinforce the dynamic, interactive nature of the competencies by examining in more detail actual examples in action in the next chapter.

Seeing the Competencies in Action

Now, let's take a look at how the seven competencies play out in four vignettes from actual leaders. Each of the leaders featured has taken a self-assessment of the seven competencies (Kirtman, 2014). The results of the self-assessment appear in the figures within each vignette.

Vignette One: The Need to Execute

One superintendent who led several districts to achieve short-term results tended to have trouble creating sustainable change. He had a history of taking over districts that were either mediocre or poor performers. He was very innovative and comfortable challenging the status quo (100 percent for competency one; see figure 3.1, page 36) in the first few months of his tenure.

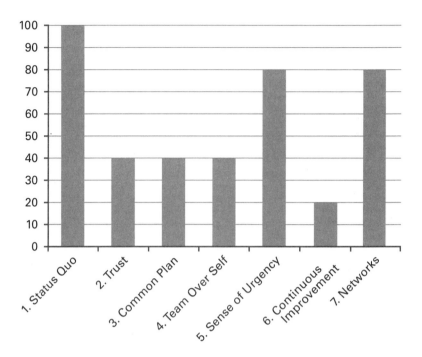

Figure 3.1: Leadership self-assessment profile—The need to execute.

He was a strong networker (80 percent for competency seven) but did not develop any long-term partnerships. His sense of urgency for change and improvement (80 percent for competency five) was very clear during his interviews for each position and his actions in his first ninety days on the job. He was not afraid of challenging the current practices that were not successful in each district. He was also skilled at evaluating staff who did not have a sense of urgency for results for students. He was able to gain the support of the school boards and most of the community who became caught up in his relentless focus on achieving results quickly for students.

The problem was that, as a leader, he was only demonstrating three of the seven competencies (one, five, and seven). While this leader did believe in focusing on team over self (40 percent for competency four), having a commonly owned plan for success (40

percent for competency three), committing to continuous improvement (20 percent for competency six), and developing trust through
clear communication and expectations (40 percent for competency
two), his impatience and inability to improve personally derailed his
efforts. He always touched on each competency but never had the
patience to allow others to learn and change. In his leadership roles,
he did work on strategic plans, but he did not focus consistently
on execution. He worked with a consultant on leadership assessments and team building with his central office team and principals.
However, the follow-up was again absent. They often did not have
sustainable results.

Overall, his inability to model leadership was very discouraging to
his team. He showed outward support to improving as a leader but
was unaware of instances that were counter to his efforts. For example, he would talk about a focus on results for student achievement
in many meetings. However, he would introduce a new initiative
without showing how it was part of the focus he had established.
In his mind, the new initiative was connected to the goals. But by
being vague with his team, the initiative countered the focus he
desired. If a team member raised a question about the new initiative,
the superintendent became defensive and accused the team member
of not being on board with the needed change. This defensiveness
made his team skeptical about the entire team-building process.
Team members were skeptical about looking honestly and openly at
their own improvement needs in an environment where their leader
lacked self-awareness. He became a "hit and run" superintendent.
He began the change process and even set high expectations for
results in each culture; however, his inability to stay focused and
concentrate on implementation resulted in short-term gains and no
sustainable improvements. Each district he led improved somewhat,
but the leaders who followed him tended to get the credit because
they focused on implementation and helped staff move through the
change process. If this superintendent used all seven competencies

in a thoughtful manner, he could have had a major impact on the districts and communities he served.

This leader was not able to develop a strong team and as a result, the direction being pursued, despite getting some good results, did not survive the appointment of a new leader. While he spoke of building a strong team, he was not able to deal effectively with feedback on his own behavior, which prevented his team from becoming a high-performance team. Since his team members never saw how their input affected his decisions, they were skeptical about spending time developing the relationships within their team that would build trust. The next superintendent who followed the one featured in this case study had his own set of priorities that set the district off in another direction.

If the district leadership team had provided feedback to this new superintendent that the lack of trust would derail results on student achievement, he could have avoided some of the setbacks that occurred in his first year. The superintendent in this example provided a coach for the high school principal. Based on the coaching, the new high school principal built a culture of trust that had been established by this superintendent but was discontinued once the next superintendent started his tenure. If there was truly a strong leadership team, which included the principals, the team would have recommended that the coach continue working with the high school principal to maintain the positive culture. However, the next superintendent did not hear any recommendation from the leadership team and subsequently discontinued the coaching of the high school principal. The lack of a strong team had a negative impact on sustainable change at the high school.

As this vignette shows, being strong, even very strong, in some dimensions (competencies one and seven) is not sufficient for great leadership.

Vignette Two: The Need for Focus

A second example concerns a principal from a charter school who had deep support from the school board, staff, and parents. The school was founded on the principle that engaging students in a learning environment with reflective listening and in-depth learning is core to its success. While test scores exist, the school uses them for learning, not just for ranking. The scores are secondary in focus to creating future citizens who are service-oriented, thoughtful learners and future leaders.

The culture of the school is nontraditional. You might see a teacher sitting on the floor discussing an issue with students in an equal partnership. You might also see students and staff having town-meeting-style discussions around current topics in the news or new ideas in education.

The principal is a thoughtful and reflective leader. He speaks softly and listens extremely well. He is calm in his demeanor and has excellent facilitative skills. He spends time with his teachers discussing how he can support them in meeting the needs of students and parents who are seen as true partners in the education process.

He exhibits many of the seven competencies in his day-to-day actions. He is all about teams and always puts team over self. He is very focused on partnerships and support networks with parents and is always increasing the number of organizations he uses to provide new learning opportunities for students and staff.

The focus of his school is on continuous learning, and he models this behavior by continually reading and reflecting on how he can improve as a leader. His school was founded on challenging the status quo and creating a true learning environment for students and not succumbing to the fast-paced world that often prevents in-depth and reflective learning. When his school completed a strategic plan, he methodically took each goal and objective and developed a work plan for success. He worked very closely with staff, the board, and parents on implementation.

Everything sounds great, right? The principal is a reflection of the culture and philosophy of the school. So what does this leader have to benefit from by applying the seven competencies to his development? He can enhance his work effectiveness if he strengthens three of the competencies that are not as strong as the other four (see figure 3.2). This principal scored an 80 percent on his self-assessment on competencies three, four, six, and seven. He rated a 60 percent on competencies one, two, and five, which indicates that improvement is needed to make this high-performing leader even better.

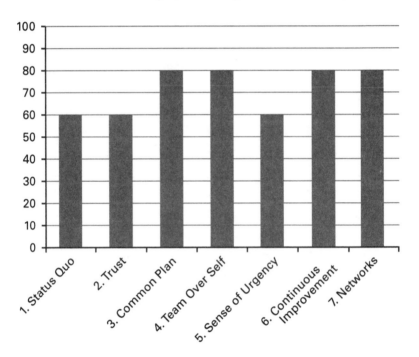

Figure 3.2: Leadership self-assessment profile—The need for focus.

While the school is a challenging-the-status-quo type of school, the principal is very compliance oriented. This style can be restrictive as he has a tendency to stay within the boundaries of the school model and philosophy. He has trouble working with faculty who buy into the school's philosophy but want to try new approaches to reach school and student goals. He is trying to manage from outcomes now rather than getting involved with how his faculty works on the goal. In other words, challenging the status quo sometimes involves focusing on actions that get results, even though strict compliance may be slightly compromised.

Competency two—"builds trust through clear communication and expectations"—is the second area for improvement. While the trust in the school is high and the expectations are clear based on their strong school model and core values, it can be difficult to directly raise tough issues and raise the bar for achievement. The principal is often hesitant in stating his vision and expectations, instead feeling that he must be more of a facilitator in the community. His leadership profile notes that his influence skills are very high, but he is low in establishing a sense of urgency for change.

Competency five—"has a high sense of urgency for change and sustainable results in improving student achievement"—is his third area for improvement. He has trouble being direct with people, which is evident to his staff. He is working with his coach to express his viewpoint at the beginning of a meeting and then use his excellent listening and analytical skills to shape the direction and strategy for discussion and action. By being more direct and focused about implementation, he will increase the speed of action and his ability to be team oriented by creating team ownership, which will increase a plan's sustainability.

The school board has challenged this principal to play more of an external role for the school. He will need to spend more time on fundraising, spearheading parent involvement, finding external partners for key elements of the strategic plan, and being more present nationally. The principal will be seeking partnerships with corporations for internships and funding for new programs, higher education for more advanced courses at the college level, and human service agencies for support on behavioral issues. His national presence will involve spreading the learnings and philosophy of the school across the nation to help students succeed in an environment of individualized learning and partnership with teachers for sustained learning. He will need to delegate more to his administrators and possibly hire a director of operations for the school.

By involving the team in the challenge of finding the right structure and distribution of responsibilities, team effectiveness and ownership of the change will increase. If the team can shift its time use to new areas and build new skills, a director of operations may not be needed. This would also save the school money. If the team finds that it cannot handle the operations role and there is a need for new staff or an operations person in the future, members will likely be more supportive of the change. The change in the principal's role will become sustainable by committing to a team-development process.

This principal has created a sense of urgency for change in a team and a process-rich environment by building his leadership team as a partner in the school's development and direction for the future.

Vignette Three: The Need for Fine-Tuning

In a third case, a superintendent of a diverse urban district that has been very successful in improving student achievement and creating a learning organization, while using the right drivers for change, can also learn from the seven competencies. This leader developed a culture of collaboration and teamwork that should sustain the results the district has achieved.

The superintendent just retired, and the assistant superintendent who supported her for many years has replaced her. The new leader is trying to carry on the excellent work that has preceded her and still find a place to establish her own identity. The retiring superintendent is extremely strong on several of the seven competencies. Her ability to put team over self is exemplary and has created a culture of learning for staff and students. The superintendent demonstrated her strong and consistent ability to challenge the status quo throughout her tenure. She went against public opinion on hiring decisions and created a focus on core values that guided everyone's practice within the district.

The district has a common plan for success that involves staff in their development and tracks progress. The changes that have occurred are a result of a sense of urgency to meet the needs of a changing demographic and the pressure to increase student achievement. The retiring superintendent is an example of a great capacity builder who created sustainable change. Therefore, it seems perfect that her successor comes from within and can carry on the vision. The situation could not be any better.

The retiring leader's competency with continuous learning as part of the culture should serve the district well. How can the new superintendent look at improvement with all this success? The new superintendent completed two leadership assessments, the Workplace Personality Inventory (WPI) and the DiSC inventory, both designed to look at behavior and compare data on high-performing leaders to this retiring superintendent. The retiring superintendent completed these assessments to help her coach the new superintendent. Some themes were immediately obvious. The new superintendent had most of the characteristics of highest-performing leaders. However, she was low in the social score of the WPI inventory, with her competency on networks and partnerships being correspondingly low. In addition, she was very inclusive and process oriented (team over self) and low on being direct about her vision of necessary improvements (builds trust through clear communication and expectations). She believed that the sense of urgency had to come from her team. She also scored high in her ability to care for others and be sensitive to personal issues (team over self).

These strong abilities to build relationships were a core strength and the hallmark of the retired superintendent. This highly effective superintendent scored 100 percent on competencies one, three, and six and an 80 percent on competencies two, four, and five (see figure 3.3, page 44). These scores should bode well for the sustainability of her improvements in the district. The scores on competencies two and four could warrant some minor action even though they are excellent, and the 60 percent on building networks and partnerships (competency seven) is an area for improvement. In regard to improving competency two, the data in Lyle's research (Kirtman, 2014) show that leaders can be overly sensitive to others' needs. This is illustrated by high-performing leaders showing lower scores on the WPI on the concern for others trait. If a leader is overly concerned, he or she might hesitate to be direct on feedback to staff on areas for improvement. When this highly successful superintendent heard the feedback on her areas for improvement, she agreed that this oversensitivity might have slowed down progress or decreased her collaboration and networking with colleagues statewide (competency seven). Sensitivity is a positive trait for support of team members and showing empathy for others. However, if a leader shows too much sensitivity and hesitates on delivering direct feedback for improvement, results can be compromised.

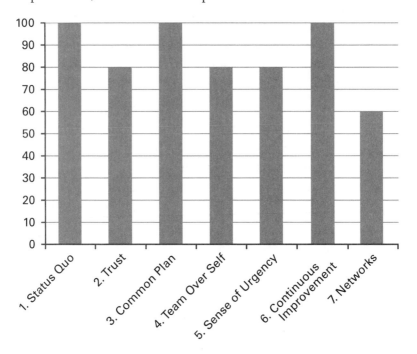

Figure 3.3: Leadership self-assessment profile—The need for fine-tuning.

The retired superintendent took on a new role as mentor to her successor. Using her network of leaders, she found a program for team development that focuses on teaching principals to provide direct critical feedback to staff for improving performance and shared this information with her successor. This process of direct feedback will maintain and even increase the trust and relationships that have been a hallmark of her leadership.

The retiring superintendent realized that she could have moved the district ahead faster with new skills; however, the foundation she established was strong for continuous improvement, and the relationships were strong enough to bring in more direct communication without compromising the relationships she already established.

Even this extraordinary leader could improve and help her successor take the district to the next level. In short, good leaders get even better by continuing to focus on all seven competencies.

Vignette Four: The Need for a Coherent Plan

A fourth example concerns a superintendent in an urban district on the West Coast of the United States who was hired to improve student achievement on test scores that had plateaued over the previous four years. The demographics in the district were changing with increased diversity, and a new sense of urgency for change was critical.

The culture of the district was very consensus based and inclusionary. The focus on process was more pronounced than the focus on results. The process focus did create a feeling of empowerment, and the administrators and teachers felt a sense of belonging and support but not necessarily a strong press for getting better results.

The new superintendent needed to come in and create a sense of urgency (competency five) and support the positive aspects of the previous culture that could be a benefit in creating sustainable change. The new superintendent had to engage in listening but also needed to find a way to create change, increase innovation, and create a results-oriented culture. His mission was to challenge the status quo and maintain the benefits of the positive culture the previous leader created.

Now, in his third year, he is trying to increase the pace of change and improvement. His leadership profile shows a results orientation and a clear emphasis on driving change at a fast pace. His profile shows he is a results-oriented person with a natural ability to challenge the status quo coupled with a personality that is very caring and sensitive to people (see figure 3.4). The team he inherited was more focused on the importance of process and consensus and incremental change.

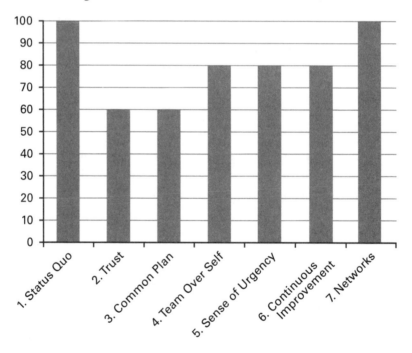

Figure 3.4: Leadership self-assessment profile—The need for a coherent plan.

The superintendent decided to focus on three competencies for change. His score on competency one ("challenges the status quo"—100 percent) was a strength for him, but his administrative team needed to embrace change. He would challenge the status quo and put a focus on team over self (competency four—80 percent). His laid-back and caring style allowed him to gain support from all internal and external constituencies. This provided social capital that allowed him to challenge current practices and make needed changes in direction and staffing. Focusing on the team allowed him to demonstrate that he did not want to be alone in driving the change process. He would create a team that would embrace the change to focus on results while preserving the aspects of the previous culture.

He used his skills on competency five (80 percent) to create a sense of urgency for change and improvement and used the past culture to help the change become sustainable by honoring practices on consensus and teamwork. Another competency to focus on was competency two—"builds trust through clear communication and expectations." His score of 60 percent indicated an area for improvement. He knew that trust was a critical aspect of the previous culture. Now, he would have to challenge the practices of the past and still maintain trust. He quickly established several approaches for communication both externally and internally. He clearly stated his vision for the district and his expectations for change. For example, he was clear on the need for a more diverse staff to mirror the changes in the student population. Being a natural extrovert, forming partnerships and networks came easy to him (100 percent on competency seven). He has been able to increase the innovation of the district through a range of partnerships.

His challenge has been in creating a commonly owned plan for success (60 percent on competency three). It was difficult to bring the culture of consensus and the culture of results together. The consensus culture created many opportunities for discussion but also an inability to be direct about what needed to improve to achieve desired results. Competency three has emerged as the perfect bridge for the two cultures. The central office and principals were struggling with having direct and honest conversations on what needed improvement. People were very indirect and not focused. There were several silos on his leadership team, and principals tended to work in isolation. The team needed one commonly owned skinny plan. The district now has a two-page plan that creates a clear sense of direction. The district has also integrated plans on technology, community and parent involvement, and innovation into the two-page plan. School-improvement plans are also being simplified into one- to two-page documents. The superintendent asked for assistance on data analysis from state and county resources, which makes life easier for principals. This creates less paperwork and more assistance on determining the most effective programs to improve student achievement.

His team is committed to learning and developing its skills on the seven competencies and is integrating the work of whole-system change into day-to-day operations. The silos are breaking down, and the focus on implementation and execution is increasing. The gap noted on the leadership profile of the central office and the principals involved the focus on implementation.

At this stage in the district's journey, the district leadership team and the principals are working on how the seven competencies can improve their individual and collective performance. The superintendent's focus on improving his score (80 percent) is a reflection of competency six—"has a commitment to continuous improvement for self and organization"—and is important for his team. The executive director of elementary education has already focused on her own improvement and has incorporated the competencies into her principals' goal setting. The executive director of secondary education has begun to integrate the seven competencies with other initiatives on innovation to simplify his principals' work. Next, the central office will incorporate the competencies into all its work and its regular district meetings and retreats.

Leading for Sustainable Success

Leaders who lead effectively are low on compliance and high on influence, team-oriented system thinkers, risk takers, network builders, and lifelong learners driven to create and sustain the highest achievement for all students. They do this by combining the seven competencies.

Now that we have seen the seven competencies in action, we can now consider what leaders need to do in order to establish focus and the conditions for sustainable success. We start with the need to change our approach to compliance so that the deep work of change can begin.

Moving Compliance to the Side of Your Plate

Ironically, many state approaches to accountability distract leaders from focusing on improvement. The Gordon Commission (2013), a group of highly respected educational leaders, drew this very conclusion: "Accountability is not the problem. The problem is that other purposes of assessment, such as providing instructionally relevant feedback to teachers, get lost when the sole goal of the state is to use them to obtain an estimate of how much students learned in the course of a year" (p. 7).

Students are born creative and curious. By the time they enter high school, however, we have removed most of the fun and excitement from their educational experience and put in its place pressure to score high on tests and prepare for the world of being serious and getting ahead. We also seem to dash the creative spirit of teachers and administrators who at one time thought they would be part of a culture immersed in the joy of learning. One superintendent in New Jersey with whom we worked shared that he was not enjoying his work and did not feel he was a leader. He felt like his real job was not superintendent but rather compliance officer.

It's true that education is serious and important, but we have lost the curiosity and excitement of learning and discovery. We have become afraid that without accountability systems our students will fail and never thrive in the real world. To the contrary, the companies that hire our graduates want curiosity, resilience, an entrepreneurial spirit, the ability to collaborate, and comfort with risk taking. What would happen with our students in schools and districts if education was enjoyable, fun, and creative and focused on developing the traits employers desire? Why do we kill the spirit of our students and administrators progressively through the education experience?

Shifting Our Focus on Accountability

Accountability has become the buzzword in education policy for closing the achievement gap. National strategy in the United States and elsewhere is to provide structure and standards to prevent schools from mishandling student education. The belief is that we cannot trust educators to make sure students learn and follow the rules that the adults have established for their own good. Wikipedia's first three words in the definition of accountability are *answerability*, *blameworthiness*, and *liability* (Accountability, n.d.). While this definition is not necessarily a reflection of policymakers' assumptions in their focus on accountability, it does expose the reality of how educators feel about the focus on accountability.

The accountability strategy is based on legitimate concerns about inconsistencies in educational delivery within and between schools, a lack of rigor in the classroom, people following rules, and an uneasiness about how resources are being allocated and their relation to results. A focus on accountability as a core improvement strategy and monitoring process for compliance sets a tone of a lack of faith and trust in the people we need (teachers and school leaders) to motivate and inspire students to learn, discover, and create.

We see the deleterious effects of increased microaccountability in the evolution of principalship—ironically in the name of instructional leadership (see Fullan, 2014). As the call for compliance increases and becomes more detailed, it becomes more and more intrusive and ineffective. We will use New Jersey as an example—it is one of a hundred or more examples we could cite. The state's policy framework starts off reasonably enough with the goal of specifying student growth objectives. Teachers are required to develop student growth objectives for each and every student, have the principal approve them and then submit them to the state. The principal then monitors individual teachers and provides annual ratings. In addition to all the work involved for teachers, this has created the new role of instructional supervisor for the district office administrators who then supervise the principal. There are not enough hours in the day to carry out these tasks, which undercut the professional relationship between principals and teachers and principals and district personnel. Richard DuFour and Robert Marzano (2009) warn us about this trend when they say, "Time devoted to the capacity of teachers to work in teams is far better spent than time devoted to observing individual teachers" (p. 67).

In short, accountability and compliance can result in educational leaders feeling restricted and constrained, which not only makes daily work ineffective but also curtails creativity and innovation. Think about the batter in baseball who feels the pressure of accountability and holds the bat too tight or the golfer tensing up on his grip on a key shot. Think of the musician who is so worried that she will play the wrong note that she loses her passion for a piece and appears mechanical while performing. The tension associated with compliance and accountability can put a focus on fear of failure. That fear will hold back a leader from the freedom to create and the willingness to try a new approach that could result in superior performance.

Can we obtain accountability with a less heavy-handed approach and improve student achievement? Accountability can be accomplished with a small but significant shift in our paradigm for creating sustainable achievement in education globally.

As Jan Sabo, assistant superintendent of academic services in the Napa Valley Office of Education, states:

> A workforce filled with people who are committed to compliance will get the job done and the results will be acceptable. But if the goal is to exceed satisfactory results and achieve excellent/superior results, commitment to the belief that all students will learn is required. (J. Sabo, personal communication, August 18, 2014)

Exemplary leadership fosters this belief. School leadership directly impacts student learning, not just test scores. Leading with trust, empowerment, and involvement while removing barriers and obstacles is an educational leader's primary role.

The problem with our obsession with accountability and compliance is illustrated through the experience of Mary, a principal in the Midwestern United States. Mary received a poor evaluation from her superintendent along with a ten-page document listing examples of her poor attitude as a leader, her negative relationships with her teachers, and her lack of support for the superintendent's policies. Beleaguered from this evaluation, Mary was told she had thirty days to respond. She sought out a coach to help her determine if she could improve as a principal or if she should resign and seek another career. She believed that it was hopeless because the superintendent had personal issues with her and was trying to document poor performance to fire her or force a resignation. She also consulted with a lawyer to see if legal action was warranted.

Mary did need to improve her relationships with her teachers and create a vision and direction for her school that motivated high performance from staff. However, the nature of the accountability approach and the following of compliance requirements from the evaluation as implemented by the superintendent created an environment that was not motivating for Mary's improvement. It was not clear if personal issues were really getting in the way of her relationship with the superintendent. However, the litigious nature of the evaluation process, which often is the result of districts focusing on compliance and accountability results, is a survival reaction to keeps one's job, not a learning opportunity.

The coach worked with Mary for eight sessions and administered a series of leadership assessments. Through the coaching, Mary changed her attitude and worked hard on improvements in her leadership style and behavior. She even began to develop a more positive relationship with the superintendent. She began to believe in herself and was reenergized. Just after she returned from a well-earned vacation, she faced another evaluation.

During the evaluation, the superintendent stated that the principal's first nine months had been terrible and that she was close to being fired. However, he noted that the last three months were very different. She was out of the woods and facing a new, positive direction. However, since the evaluation was for a year, and he could not trust that she would maintain her progress, he still rated her as unsatisfactory. He believed that she only improved because of his punitive approach. For example, the superintendent believed that the principal was micromanaging her staff. Therefore, he agreed to meet with staff members separately without her present to make sure they felt supported. While he was correct that the staff felt micromanaged, his accountability focus did not explore why Mary was micromanaging; he just solved the problem himself without coaching Mary on how she could build a trust relationship with her staff. His fear-based approach of using words such as *terrible* and *ineffective leadership* was punitive and not conducive to learning. Therefore, while the problems were real and needed attention, his accountability approach translated into a legal response from Mary to hire a lawyer. If the superintendent put aside compliance and accountability, the approach would have resulted in Mary improving her leadership in a manner in which she felt supported. The coach provided a motivating and reflective process, not an accountability and compliance effort, resulting in her improved leadership behavior.

When Mary discussed the evaluation with her coach, she felt demoralized. The superintendent did not recognize that motivation and her new attitudes and skills were the reason the last three months were better. While she did recognize that the poor evaluation is what got her attention, it was the positive coaching and her hard work toward change that improved her performance. In fact, the fear her superintendent expressed and the pressure needed to continue to maintain progress demonstrated the downside of a culture of accountability and compliance.

Mary was putting much effort into coaching because she wanted to succeed. The superintendent, mired in his evaluation forms and wanting to be punitive, missed the purpose of evaluation. He should have been looking for her improved performance and finding ways to reward and recognize progress. Mary continued to improve despite the evaluation process because of her self-motivation and the support of her coach and colleagues. Remember, fear may get someone's attention to inspire change, but motivation is the reason sustainable improvements occur.

Proposing a New Paradigm for Accountability

We propose a new paradigm for accountability: creating exciting, engaging environments that are focused on results where accountability is a byproduct, not a goal. Todd Sumner, principal of the Francis W. Parker Charter Essential School in Devens, Massachusetts, supports and is committed to working with the state's accountability system on teacher evaluation and special education response to intervention (RTI). He believes the key elements of the state accountability system are helpful to his school because they ensure the school has the structures in place for a comprehensive system to educate all students. However, Todd has figured out how to be accountable and compliant in a manner that is motivating and engaging. He adapted Massachusetts's accountability audit requirements but translated them into an approach to match his school's culture and environment. He has turned the accountability statement into two essential discussion questions for all constituencies within the school. He has ongoing discussions with staff, administrators, and parents on what is the proper balance between heterogeneous and individual learning. Instead of putting in systems and structures to implement compliance requirements, he engages his community in a genuine learning process that provides an approach to consistency that is core to their mission and practice: creating individual learning opportunities for students and staff.

Todd is using the right driver—collaboration—to focus on results and building social capital that will make the accountability effort engaging and motivating. His approach will make accountability stick because the group is helping the group succeed.

Todd is also focusing on becoming a high-performing leader by working from several of the seven competencies for high-performing leaders. He is challenging the status quo in the school by replacing the individual philosophy of educating students with the collective responsibility of developing schoolwide strategies that impact all students. He is also building trust through clear communication and expectations by using the state standards to establish a set of expectations for students and staff. Todd is also focusing on team over self—a key strategy for engaging all constituencies in the discussion.

Accountability is important if it is a subset of a focus on results and a team process for motivation. A true motivational environment that is obsessed and vigilant about results for students will never have a problem with accountability. As one excellent retired special education teacher, Gail Feldman, said, "I do not understand why there is all this focus on accountability for teachers" (G. Feldman, personal communication, July 7, 2014). She shared that she is accountable for her students' learning every day—she does not need an outside rubric to hold her accountable.

Doesn't true accountability come from within? While it seems easier to use external, top-down accountability processes to achieve sustainable results, it will never work on a larger scale to improve the whole system. Those who support and advocate for accountability and compliance say there isn't time to motivate enough people to get results and be self-accountable. They believe that it would take years to find high-quality leaders and that accountability is a faster way to results. What we propose, however, increases internal accountability and reinforces it with transparent external accountability. Let's explore what it would be like to push compliance and externally driven accountability to the side of the plate and find out how a school or district can create an exciting, motivating environment for results.

Karen Rue, superintendent of Northwest Independent School District in Fort Worth, Texas, has shifted the paradigm of accountability and compliance in her district. For Karen, compliance—laws, rules, and regulations—looms, but it never leads. Rue observes that her district has developed a culture of continuous improvement that focuses on preparing students with high levels of academic strength including content literacy, digital skills, critical-thinking skills, problem-solving skills, and collaboration and communication. Students must be future ready, with confidence in their ability to tackle or think through and adapt to what life will throw their way. Compliance is at the bottom of the list in their efforts to create innovation in learning. If a rule gets in the way of something important, they simply find another way to get what needs doing done.

A principal in one urban district met a very distraught student who had lost his school-issued laptop computer. The cost of a new computer was prohibitive for the student and his family. The district office said there was nothing that could be done to get a new computer for this student. The principal would not accept no for an answer on this issue because a laptop was critical for the student's education. She looked into the insurance policy that the district held on technology equipment and found a way to put a claim in for a lost computer. But there was one last challenge: there was a $200 deductible for the new computer. The student still could not afford the cost, so the principal arranged a payment plan with the district to pay the $200. This payment plan also emphasized to the student that responsibility to keep track of valuable equipment was very important. The principal would not allow a rule to be a deterrent to student learning. She worked creatively to solve the problem and still taught the student about personal responsibility.

If we changed our conversations with staff and students to say, "I believe in you" and "You can accomplish extraordinary results," would that improve student achievement and staff performance? While fear and critical feedback motivate some people, encouragement and support motivate the vast majority of people to succeed (see especially Fullan's [2015] analysis of the role of feedback for growth). Those who support accountability might say that telling people who are not performing that they can achieve and you believe in them will not be enough to improve their achievement. We agree that just being positive and motivating alone will not work. Experiencing what success looks and feels like and understanding the skills and knowledge required to reach one's dreams are major parts of the formula for success. Our new paradigm of creating cultures of excitement, creativity, and motivation includes the need for leaders to provide critical feedback to students and staff to help them achieve extraordinary results.

Critical feedback can motivate people to reach their goals. In an environment where there is an excitement for learning and obtaining desired results, people become motivated to learn and improve. They are not afraid of failure and are willing to take risks. They also want to move beyond failing to achieve success to gain a feeling of accomplishment for their hard work. The best leaders want critical feedback so they can improve. They do not fear it but crave it!

Finding the Time

You might ask how leaders will have time to create environments filled with excitement, creativity, and motivation. First, let's consider the amount of time leaders spend on compliance tasks. Policymakers and state and federal workers, who are often removed from the real world of schools, develop these tasks. In many cases, they have never been in schools and do not understand the impact of their requirements on the educators charged with improving student achievement. Filling out forms, documenting activities, gathering evidence, writing reports, and drafting updates take away time from the work of creating innovative learning environments.

It is helpful to consider how corporations such as Amazon, Google, Facebook, and Apple handle compliance. In fact, unlike education, corporations such as these are not inundated with compliance activities—they are too focused on getting results and meeting and exceeding customer needs for compliance work to distract them. These companies do have to deal with compliance requirements for hiring, tax laws, equal employment opportunity practices, disclosure information, and so on. However, this compliance work is not the focus of their leaders.

In most innovative companies, compliance is part of management. For example, one of the most innovative companies in the world, the Walt Disney Company, has as a core value: "fanatical attention to consistency and detail" (Collins & Porras, 2002). This supports two of their other values, which are "happiness to millions" and "creativity, dreams, and imagination." Disney's focus on consistency and detail allows it to meet its compliance requirements (such as park cleanliness) while being innovative and creative.

A manager must set up systems for reporting, monitoring results, filing documents, and other operational tasks required to run and maintain a business. Managers usually do these tasks efficiently in a minimal amount of time. Education, by contrast, has minimized the importance of good management. In the effort to focus on instructional leadership, management has become a lost art in education.

But it is not possible for a leader to be successful without possessing strong management skills in financial management, project management, forecasting, and data analysis. These skills are all critical to turn goals and innovations into sustainable results.

We propose moving the focus from accountability and compliance in education to broad-based leadership and sound management practices. If a principal has a strong support staff that can deliver reports on time and provide timely data needed for planning, he or she will be a better leader.

We seem to be saying that adding time for management training to the overwhelming tasks that educational leaders are facing will save time. How is that possible? The reason is that accountability and compliance will not be the main work of leaders. Shifting their focus in such a way frees up time for leaders to help develop capacities that have greater impact. These leaders move their focus from fighting internal battles for meeting external requirements to building innovative, motivating cultures that are based on results and continuous improvement. Learning how to manage will prevent compliance requirements from interfering with leaders' work.

We must make this shift now because accountability and compliance requirements are getting worse every year. For example, some compliance requirements originate from a problem that has occurred in one school, so the state must require all schools to adopt new practices to prevent the problem from occurring in all schools. A great example are the U.S. policies regarding school safety, such as a zero-tolerance policy that leads to blind compliance without considering the individual situations (for example, a kindergartener bringing a toy sword to school and the child being suspended or expelled). Are these policies and plans the answer to stopping bullying? We argue that building a positive school culture and relationships between adults and students are more important. The policies are helpful but not a panacea. One school guidance counselor in an urban district reflected on the Columbine tragedy by commenting that all schools' work after Columbine was about security and protocols for safety.

While that is a natural reaction to a tragedy of that magnitude, little, if any, time was put into discussing how schools reach out to all students and find ways to connect to students on the fringe. Security is not a true comprehensive prevention strategy for these terrible events.

The shift of accountability and compliance tasks means that this work is still important but not the work of effective leaders. Often these tasks, if necessary, can be delegated to staff to free up the principal or superintendent to lead. In effect, leaders who move compliance to the side of the plate in order to focus on instruction and student achievement do a variety of things to blunt the distraction of excessive accountability requirements: they find minimal ways to handle bureaucratic demands by selectively ignoring some requirements, by becoming efficient at handling administrative matters, by delegating to other staff routine requests, and so on. They get away with this, so to speak, because they score high on student achievement.

Building Strong Self-Management Skills to Create More Time for Leadership

The most innovative leaders who are not overwhelmed and mired in compliance tasks are both good managers and have excellent self-management skills and systems. If you are a leader who is running around feeling stressed responding to all the day-to-day battles, your self-management skills could be a part of the problem.

James Lister, executive director of the Plummer Home in Salem, Massachusetts, states, "Ask all candidates for a leadership role to describe his or her personal management system for tracking tasks and meeting deadlines in the first interview. The reason for this question is that one cannot lead consistently if one cannot keep track of priorities, manage important commitments, and respond quickly to calls and emails from constituents" (J. Lister, personal communication, April 22, 2014).

If a leader is spending each day just reacting, he or she cannot begin to think and act strategically. The people who continually say they are so busy are not the leaders we want in the 21st century. It is clear that the best leaders are not too busy to think strategically and be receptive to a new idea or opportunity. These leaders are grounded in their role to lead, not react, and to build capacity for goal attainment, by not doing all the work themselves. A leader's job is not to *do* tasks; it is to build capacity to help others complete results-oriented responsibilities.

To begin to free up time to lead, take out your calendar, and eliminate five hours per week of tasks that are not results oriented. Stephen Covey's (1989) four quadrants for leaders (figure 4.1) can be a great guide for this exercise. He provides a way to graphically organize tasks: (1) tasks that are urgent and important, (2) tasks that are not urgent but important, (3) tasks that are urgent and not important, and (4) tasks that are not urgent and not important.

1 Urgent Important	2 Not Urgent Important
3 Urgent Not Important	4 Not Urgent Not Important

Figure 4.1: Covey's (1989) four quadrants.

Covey (1989) says that your work as a leader should be in quadrants 1 and 2, the urgent and important and not urgent and important. Quadrants 3 and 4 are the tasks that distract leaders. Quadrant 2 is preferred because it could involve creating a vision for your school, determining strategies for engaging parents in the education process, and coaching teachers. Quadrant 1 is also important because it allows time for responding to safety issues and students', teachers', and colleagues' needs. The not urgent and not important tasks in quadrant 4 are the areas you should delegate or try to resist completely. The urgent and not important tasks in quadrant 3 are traps for crisis management.

One very innovative superintendent discovered that his leadership team was feeling stressed. He had created a vibrant district focused on the joy of learning and realizing great results. However, while he was moving compliance to the side of his plate and creating many new opportunities for innovation, his team still felt overwhelmed. He asked team members to cut five hours per week of tasks that were not results oriented from their schedules. In many cases, the tasks were self-imposed and could be easily eliminated. For example, one principal admitted that he spent several hours each week editing his staff's documents. He could reduce this time by trusting his team more and providing coaching on writing skills. However, the administrators could not remove all five hours by just focusing on their own self-management. After more reflection, the principals noted a systemwide time problem: all principals had to attend every school board meeting (two meetings per month for a total of eight hours). This left them tired from long nights and frustrated by spending less time with their families.

The superintendent agreed to talk to the school board about this issue. He took the opportunity to recognize the great work of his team publicly and explained that changing the attendance policy would increase the productivity of his leaders by giving them more personal time, making the point that the work-life balance is key to successful leadership. This resulted in the decision that principals only had to attend a school board meeting if their school was on the agenda.

Another principal in an underperforming high school has stellar leadership skills, but he can't reach his potential because he is so reactive to every call from the central office and every incident in his school. He continually leaves strategic meetings to respond to a problem or return each central office call immediately. His coach, a former high school principal of thirty years, commented that he feels like he is in an air traffic control room when he meets with this principal. The coach began shadowing this talented but reactive principal to show him how to lead, not react.

For example, the principal did all the morning announcements himself. He believed that this illustrated his leadership and hands-on approach to staff and students. However, as his coach pointed out, students and staff rarely paid any attention to the announcements. The coach helped the principal slow down and think about what he was doing and why. He was reacting to the need to show his superintendent that he was connecting to students and staff. This symptomatic and reactive action was not effective in meeting his goals. A more strategic idea would be to have a student make the morning announcements.

This principal was also always behind on tasks and deadlines. The self-management process to improve this problem was to engage the assistant principal in a process to list and manage tasks and projects. Using a whiteboard, they now list all the projects and deadlines, and the assistant principal makes sure all deadlines are completed, leaving the principal more time to coach teachers on instructional issues. The assistant principal was able to track and follow up on tasks easily within his work day rather than spending more time fixing the problems that resulted from previous poor follow-through on work assignments.

Since education involves customer service, responding to customers or people who can influence the work in a school is critical. Making sure that callers receive a response in twenty-four hours is very important. Not responding has a negative effect on forming your support network. (The concept of forming a broad support network is explored in chapter 7, page 107.) Although an innovative leader realizes that almost everyone can be a resource, he or she does not drop everything when a call or email comes in. These leaders work out a system with their support staff to respond. A quick email can acknowledge the correspondence. A call from the office staff saying that the principal is in meetings and can respond early next week can help the caller feel that there is interest in his or her point of view. The goodwill of showing people you care about them and are interested in what they have to say is the basis of creating a positive culture.

Opportunities come to those who can engage quickly. An example of this is a superintendent who did not return the call of a technology company looking to provide $100,000 in grants for innovation in teaching, which resulted in the money being offered to another district. Another superintendent who spent all his time managing compliance and accountability tasks from the state due to the school being designated as underperforming did not have time to return a foundation's calls giving his district over $300,000 per year for science education. This district may lose the funding to a charter school in the same community that does have time to communicate with the foundation. In these examples, the leaders' lack of response to key strategic issues due to a lack of delegating tasks, such as returning calls, resulted in major problems or a loss of an opportunity that would have helped the district or school meet its goals.

The pressures of accountability and compliance have resulted in many leaders, especially in urban districts that have more direct crisis on a day-to-day basis that can detract from a focus on teaching and learning, becoming reactive. In trying to meet everyone's needs and demands, leaders have very little time and energy to develop a strong plan for results.

Establishing a Results-Based Culture

Pedro Galaviz, superintendent of Canutillo Independent School District in El Paso, Texas, is turning around his school district's culture through establishing a results-based culture focused on student learning. He is putting his focus on building the skills of his staff to become high-performance leaders and to make self-reflection part of their everyday life. Pedro is a true model of learning and leadership. He reads voraciously about the art and science of leadership and is including his team in his vehement desire to improve and continuously learn. He is creating a dream and vision for excellence in his district when the belief in the community is that limited resources and compliance requirements to meet accountability are the focus. He is replacing the fear of not meeting compliance requirements with a passion to succeed. Pedro makes sure some staff are focused on compliance; however, it is no longer the focus of every conversation. Learning, student dreams, and the staff feeling passion and excitement for being a part of something special are the new foci.

Marinel McGrath, the superintendent in Andover, Massachusetts, is also a lifelong learner who is committed to continuously learning about leadership. Marinel, when faced with a cumbersome evaluation process involving the school board, built a strong partnership and new model for evaluation. She shifted the paradigm so it was no longer the school board's responsibility to evaluate the superintendent and to hold her accountable; its new job was to work to help the superintendent succeed.

Marinel's state system had several goals, rubrics for evaluation, and requirements to make sure the superintendent showed evidence of improvement. However, no one ever asked the question: "Is this the way a superintendent should be evaluated?" CEOs in other fields are evaluated on results, not on an inordinate number of goals and detailed evidence of completing activities. Superintendents have always tried to stop their boards from micromanaging; now the state has institutionalized micromanagement by requiring school boards to watch over and gather evidence that the superintendent is doing her job.

The Andover School Board has agreed that it wants to be strategic and not micromanage the superintendent. To achieve this, evaluation now has goals in the following three areas.

1. Increasing innovation throughout the district to improve student achievement and provide new opportunities for staff and students

2. Building the leadership capacity of principals to create sustainable learning environments

3. Increasing community engagement to build support for district goals

Marinel works with the board and her staff on strategies to meet her goals that ultimately affect student achievement. They do not spend hours on training for the evaluation process or discussing the minute details and evidence of what Marinel is doing on a daily basis. Instead, they discuss challenges, strategies to reach goals, and what the board can do to help with resource allocation, partnerships, and contacts from within the community or from their personal and business networks.

Focusing on Compliance Tasks That Matter

With this new paradigm, the leader is freed from time spent on compliance tasks—but that doesn't mean the tasks don't still need to be completed. Many leaders have tried to challenge their state and the federal government, spending inordinate amounts of time on committees designed to streamline government, decrease the focus on inputs and move time to outputs, and to make myriad other attempts to minimize bureaucracy in America. Most of these efforts have been futile and fall by the wayside as administrations change and new issues emerge, and all the while the bureaucracies have continued creating more and more regulations and requirements.

If you want to save time and build your innovative and creative results-oriented culture, stop fighting city hall; the return on your time investment is rarely worth it. The new paradigm frees your time spent on meaningless tasks if you understand one important thing: you do not have to get an A in all compliance requirements—a grade of C will suffice. This is a tough concept to grasp for educators who always want an A in everything. Remember that compliance is often about meeting the minimum requirements, not getting a perfect score. Some educators are calling this concept *creative insubordination*—the act of not blindly following a rule when it is stated from a higher source—because it allows us to control our time and priorities without being insubordinate. While most people would agree that the act of being creative and thoughtful in how you interpret a rule is preferable, others do assume that a rule must be followed without question.

For example, one high school principal who was about to retire wanted to create a legacy in her school. When asked how she would accomplish this, she said she wanted all her teacher evaluations completed in a thorough manner and filed in proper folders to meet all state requirements. She indicated she spent eight hours on each evaluation. But was this action of filing evaluations a high-leverage strategy for maintaining a legacy?

By discussing results and creating a fun and vibrant school, the principal decided she could spend at least four hours coaching each teacher on his or her goals and dreams. Helping teachers improve their practice by learning from her experience was much more valuable to her legacy than a written document in a file. Spending four hours on an evaluation form was not an A effort for this principal; however, she was willing to sacrifice the A to spend time with her teachers. The results were an A for the teachers and completed state requirements.

Sometimes administrators do need to get an A in compliance requirements. If the requirement is not key to a result, however, then a C is more than enough, especially if it is accompanied by an A for teacher development and student learning. Tasks that require an A involve completing individual education plans (IEPs) within state requirements, sending in accurate reports to the IRS, and meeting safety regulations.

Begin by making a list of all compliance requirements: state, federal, and district. Make two columns. The first column should list the requirements that are critical for you to meet your goals for student achievement. The second column is the list of requirements that you can afford to get a C in. Make sure you review your decisions with your supervisor before you move ahead. Now, delegate the C items to support staff and your leadership team. You can have the final approval, but do not spend time writing the first draft of the reports.

One principal with whom we worked expressed doubt that this process would work. He described an example from his school: he designated a staff member to press a button to let people into the building. This staff member was out, so the principal had to spend the whole day pressing the button because, he claimed, security and safety are so important. Yes, security and safety are critical goals for all schools; however, this is a demonstration of poor management. Good management is about creating systems for getting work done. This includes having backup systems when the original system does not work. Not many people would argue that the principal was the only one who could have pressed the button.

This example shows how many of us are stuck mindlessly completing compliance tasks. Time is an extremely important commodity. We cannot afford to waste it on work that has no bearing on results. Time is also important to compliance regulators. We urge you to get compliance tasks finished and submitted early. If you submit a form to the state early, you get a great benefit. If you miss something or need to be more thorough, the regulators are often very helpful in pointing out any mistakes, helping you meet the requirements in an efficient manner. Even if you have additional work to do, it will usually be minimal and not as arduous as the time and effort you would have spent on an A effort.

This strategy of making time to lead is helping many educational leaders free up their time to focus on what should really matter in their districts and schools, such as implementing goals on innovation, capacity building, and community engagement, which are all in service of creating sustainable improvements in student achievement.

Using Your New Time Effectively

The tasks associated with a compliance culture are very narrow and tactical. They are not strategic, high-impact work. Compliance is mired in tasks that are not inspirational and are devoid of new opportunities for learning; as we've shown, leaders with a compliance mentality are often reactive, not proactive. Tracking how many people have completed their evaluations leaves very little time to ponder the question about why people are not completing their evaluations. Achieving mere compliance, in other words, is a low-yield way for leaders to spend their time. The seven competencies outlined in chapter 2 give you a direction for the skills and behaviors that get the best results. For example, building external networks and partnerships (such as with a community agency to address students' behavioral issues or a business that can provide ideas and resources for an innovative idea to improve mathematics scores) or focusing on team over self to improve your school's capacity are ventures for high-yield results.

Leadership team meetings are supposed to be strategic in nature; they should focus on identifying problems and patterns in the organization and determining high-impact strategies to change behavior and create innovative methods to get results. Leadership meetings should be about external data and trends and shifts in high-impact areas that affect education. One high school principal tried to add strategic thinking to his meetings with his deans of discipline. These deans were increasing school suspensions every year based on a rigid application of school policies. The deans did not see their role as connected to student achievement. They said that was the teacher's job, and they rarely talked to teachers. The principal helped turn the discussions into a strategic focus on results, which led to a discovery that the same students were being suspended over and over again. Actually, the students were also coming from the same classrooms and teachers.

The strategic question was explored, What if the focus of the deans was on teaching and learning and not on discipline? One dean panicked and said that this challenged his whole definition of his purpose in the school. What would it mean to focus on teaching and learning? The principal raised the question that it would be great to bring the deans into a room with the teachers so that everyone could own the process of refocusing from discipline to teaching and learning.

The principal was smart enough to point out the fear that this combined meeting would create. He knew that the school's culture would indicate that this would be a meeting to place blame. He engaged the deans in a conversation about how to make this a team-oriented, empowering effort. The results were fantastic, and the deans were able to work with the teachers and decrease the need for suspensions.

Strategic thinking requires one to step back, think, and analyze. Accountability and compliance result in fast actions that are often reactive. Strategic thinking allows one to decrease the number of tasks for high impact. The meeting with the deans and the teachers was a high-impact meeting. This also resulted in the deans joining the school's leadership team to capture their perspective in broad discussion on school goals and practices.

Bringing Innovative Leadership to Your School or District

You have simplified your environment (chapter 1) and moved the compliance issues to the side. There is now room to bring in innovative leadership to your school and district. While instructional leadership is important and a key for education, it is too narrow a focus for leaders. There needs to be a broader definition of leaders' actions as noted in the seven competencies. If the focus is only on instruction, there leaves very little room for other forms of leadership. Innovation is not a separate strand of leadership; it needs to be intertwined with educational leaders' role and actions.

Brett Kustigian, a superintendent in Warren, Massachusetts, in a small rural district, presented a vision to his community that his district will become one of the most innovative school districts in the United States. How can this little district of only three schools make such a claim? Brett says that he must think big and bold and reach out to any and all partners to provide the best for every student. In Brett's words, "I have no choice" (B. Kustigian, personal communication, September 5, 2014).

In fact, Brett does have a choice—he just *chose* to act differently. He could be like many small rural districts that live in a world that has very few resources, no industry, a small tax base, and an old-fashioned conventional thinking and try to do the best he can. Brett, who is one of the youngest superintendents in Massachusetts, is always open to new ideas and innovation. He has partnerships with universities, community agencies, national organizations, and anyone he can work with to help provide opportunities for his students.

Brett has made each one of the three schools in his district an innovation school. This allows him by state law to remove some of the restrictions of compliance that are part of traditional schools. This gives Brett and his principals room to breathe, innovate, and thrive. He has made his district a STEAM (science, technology, engineering, arts, and mathematics) district and is providing opportunities for experiential learning for all K–12 students. Brett has formed a unique partnership with his school board and has invested in leadership and innovation training for his leadership team. He wants everyone to be part of the dream for all the students in this poor rural community.

Brett does not spend his time on compliance. He delegates work, uses technology to streamline his processes, and does not sweat the small stuff. If you call Brett, he often responds in minutes, not hours, and is excited about any new idea that can help his district. He is able to respond quickly to strategic opportunities because he delegates all other tasks effectively. He has also been able to develop a skinny plan for his district to focus his work on high-impact initiatives. Brett is very strategic as he works hard on creating opportunities for economic development in his communities. He sees his role as a leader in the community, not just for the schools. Brett focuses on the right drivers and works on developing his competencies to be a better leader every day. The governor has awarded his district state grants, and national magazines, such as *U.S. News & World Report* (2012 Silver Medal), have recognized the amazing increase in advanced placement (AP) courses for a district with almost no resources.

Can you imagine if all superintendents were open to new ideas and spent their time on creating vibrant environments? As Patrick Sweeney, the superintendent of the Napa Valley Unified School District, says:

> I must provide the creativity and innovation environment for our staff and students to match the energy of our world today. I am OK taking risks for our students and learning from our failures. I have built a strong relationship with our community and I am confident that they will support us because they know we are committed to every child. (P. Sweeney, personal communication, July 17, 2014)

Knowing This Will Work

The research that Lyle (Kirtman, 2014) has conducted on over one thousand educational leaders has demonstrated that the highest results come from the leaders who are low on compliance and rule following and high on innovation. Unfortunately, the data also show that districts are not hiring innovative leaders; they are hiring leaders who have, at best, a superficial sense of urgency for results (get results but don't upset the bureaucracy), are highly compliant, are low risk takers, and often too top-down in their leadership style. The data on the high-performing leaders indicate that they are creative and innovative, partnership and team driven, persuasive, influence oriented, and able to provide clear and direct feedback on performance.

Therefore, we must change our hiring and professional development processes. This must begin by educating the school boards about what types of leaders are successful. They seem to hire conservatively or too bold and top down. As Kirtman (2014) has found, the tendency of school boards to hire top-down leaders in order to get new results almost always fails as new leaders come and go. If the boards understand who they should be hiring to lead their districts, and then these superintendents in turn hire the right administrators and principals, we can change the cultures of our educational system.

It will take courage to move against the tide with our hiring and professional development efforts to create vibrant environments in our districts and nationally. It will also be important to bring in external partners, such as business and industry, community development groups, medical organizations, and the nonprofit community, to help us change our focus. These fields have had to change and can help us anticipate problems and learn from their mistakes and success stories. Leaders must take the reins in their own districts and schools and bring their communities along for the ride.

Using Social Media for Positive Change

We must also remember that we have a tool that can change the landscape and move mountains for our schools: social media. Social media has influenced public policy, helped elect U.S. President Barack Obama, and created a powerful force in the world. Educators are very slow to the social media world, fearing that they will get themselves or others in trouble. The fears of interacting with students and loosening boundaries have made leaders reluctant. Boundaries with students are important, but once again, the fear has overtaken the benefit. Social media can become part of a strategy to educate the public and broaden our support networks. We must use the powerful force of social media to get the message out to the public on what we want to create in our schools.

We can bring community members and the quiet, supportive parents into our conversations through social media. Social media is influencing elections for school boards, allowing for special interest parents to win elections on single issues. Recently, in a school district on the east coast of the United States, a parent with advanced technology skills was able to win a position on the school board by exclusively using social media and not attending meetings or making any personal appearances to campaign. If we engage in social media, we can educate communities on districts' needs and inform them of our excitement in re-engaging in our most treasured resources: our schools and our students.

Steven Stone, a superintendent in Dracut, Massachusetts, and strong introvert, has used social media (Twitter and LinkedIn) to reach out in his community and create a broad-based dialogue on educational excellence. Being an introvert presented a challenge to Steve as he was not as comfortable spending time externally in a range of social situations. Although he did connect with the community in person, social media has helped him extensively and to exceed the board's expectations. His board cited him for his excellent skills in reaching out to the community. Not bad for an introvert!

Celebrating Your Results and Accomplishments

Instead of starting your meetings with a dull list of work and tasks that need to be done, begin by talking about what is making you feel good about your work. When you talk about what you've accomplished or the one moment of insight about your students that made you think differently, your excitement becomes contagious.

We are not being Pollyanna and saying everything is wonderful and that reality is not important. Reality, tasks, problems, and mistakes will always find their place. However, showing positive feelings from having self-worth, contributing, and making a difference are being preempted by a compliance regime in which you get no satisfaction and no results. Try it! Start your meeting with some positives, thank someone with a personal handwritten note, tell someone he or she did a good job, and relay student or staff stories about making critical changes and reaching extraordinary goals.

The message of this chapter is to deliberately reduce the amount of time you spend on managerial compliance and repurpose that time in the service of learning that gets results. You and your system will become more powerful in every way. Free yourself from low-yield tasks, and increase your time on activities that generate results. You and your district will end up being much more energized.

Staying Focused

We just explained how successful educational leaders repurpose their time away from mundane compliance toward continuous improvement. In this chapter, we provide two very clear examples of what this looks like, not only for individual schools, but also for districts. In these two cases, the districts operated from 2004 to 2013 during a period that was heavily overlaid with system compliance requirements.

Distractions, such as mandates or interesting innovations, can keep schools and districts constantly off balance—and that does seem to be the case in most jurisdictions. But feeling off balance is not inevitable. Figuring out our priorities, making them coherent, and then staying the course is a tall but not impossible order. Staying purposefully focused is the route to success in uncertain environments.

In this chapter, we explore two districts in California that started at or near the bottom of the heap in student performance, and despite the constant influx of high-poverty English learner immigrants, moved steadily and dramatically to become well above the state average in effectiveness. They began to get results within two years, steadily improved over a ten-year period, and are still going strong. One district is Garden Grove Unified School District in Orange County, which is south of Los Angeles; the other, Sanger Unified School District, is in the Central Valley area. Michael knows both districts well and has worked with them (after they obtained initial success). We have the additional advantage of drawing on external researchers' accounts, who wrote third-party reports on how the districts evolved since 2004 (for Garden Grove, see Knudson, 2013; for Sanger, see David & Talbert, 2013). Two stories, one theme—what does staying focused look like in complex times, and how was it done? Incidentally staying focused, by definition, means that the explanations for success will be small in number—get a few core things right, in concert, and relentlessly pursue and refine them.

Garden Grove

Garden Grove has just under fifty elementary schools and about twenty intermediate and high schools. The increasingly diverse student population is 47,600 with 86 percent Latino and Asian and an average poverty rate of 72 percent. In 2004, the percentage of high school graduates meeting state standards at 24 percent was well below the state and Orange County averages; by 2012, it reached 50 percent—well above the state (38 percent) and Orange County (43 percent) averages. In elementary English language and mathematics proficiency, Garden Grove moved steadily up over the decade, eventually performing at or above its highest-performing urban peers (Knudson, 2013).

Laura Schwalm was superintendent during this entire period and built what is quintessentially a stay-focused culture. As Joel Knudson (2013) describes it, Garden Grove's success boils down to six interrelated elements that have become part of its deep culture—the Garden Grove way—as its members often describe.

1. The centrality of students and teachers

2. Coherence

3. Emphasis on relationships

4. A central office service mentality

5. Trust and empowerment

6. An orientation to continuous improvement

Overall focus does not come from doing one or two things in isolation. It comes from a set—albeit a reasonably small set, given the complexity of change—of six key factors. First, Garden Grove is relentlessly committed to student success and to the success of its teachers. It realizes that you cannot have one without the other. In our own workshops, we sometimes observe that almost everyone will agree that all students can learn, but not as many will readily agree that all teachers can learn. Once you acknowledge that teaching and learning are central to both students and teachers, you must make it a reality. Because Garden Grove holds the learning of students and adults as central, it knows that it can't just focus on test results. You must focus on quality instruction—in fact, on *shared quality instruction*. The hard part of focus is that it must become shared across a very large number of teachers—in this case, in around seventy highly diverse schools. The question then becomes what else must be done to ensure widespread and deep quality instruction.

Embracing the first factor—the centrality of students and teachers—does not amount to much unless you have accompanying strategies to act on it. *Coherence*, the second factor, is a good word for the themes in this book. It is not just alignment in which the elements of curriculum, instruction, assessment, professional development, finance, and so on are abstractly aligned but rather how individuals and groups experience these components day after day. In this regard, Garden Grove leaders are focused on identifying and spreading the best (with evidence) ideas and practices across the system. The issue is not where the ideas come from—top, bottom, sideways—but what are the effective ideas, and how can they become widespread? In many ways, coherence is at the heart of the change process, and we do not underestimate the difficulty in achieving it. For one thing, the other five factors in Garden Grove's culture all contribute to reinforcing a growing coherence in the culture about quality instructional practices.

Let's express this in change-process terms. Effective change processes shape and reshape quality ideas as they build capacity and ownership over time. Change is a process, not an event. We will also show how collaboration or teamwork contributes to focus and coherence. The bottom line, as superintendent Laura Schwalm explains is, "If you want to move something that's difficult to move, everyone needs to be pushing in the same direction [otherwise] very good people can build very effective silos" (as cited in Knudson, 2013, p. 10).

Another reinforcing element in the culture is the emphasis on relationships, the third factor. The first aspect is the care paid to hiring people and the personal attention they receive on many fronts welcoming them to the Garden Grove culture. From day one, people feel valued by the organization and by peers and district leaders. But note this personal touch plays itself out in the context of the other five factors, which link personal value with the content of the work.

Knudson (2013) calls the fourth factor a central office service mentality. Having worked in Garden Grove since 2013, Michael believes that this is actually a blend of pressure and support. Support is provided, but it is in the service of quality instruction and student performance. Laura Schwalm puts it this way: "If we as leaders are not helping everyone become smarter and better, we're not doing our job" (as cited in Knudson, 2013, p. 12). Because the work is so thoroughly interactive, horizontally and vertically, pressure and support become seamless to the culture.

The fifth factor is trust and empowerment. This has been a gradual development. At the beginning, there was a lot more push from the district to focus on student quality instruction. As this developed, and as teacher capacity (individually and in teams) increased, there was much more openness to ideas from peers at the school level and at the level of coaches who work with schools. Trust and empowerment do not mean leaving people alone but rather relying on people as a source of valuable ideas for the group. Such teamwork generates more ideas and serves as a process to sort out good from not-so-good ideas, retaining the ideas that are most effective. Good collaboration of this kind reduces bad variation. In other words, because there is a strong focus, and because people interact over the practices that will best contribute to quality instruction, greater consistency of instructional practices evolves.

Finally, while good collaboration reduces bad (ineffective) variation, there is still a press toward continuous improvement—using corresponding evidence that inspires the group to consider new, potentially more-effective practices.

The problem in most districts is that instructional practices are all over the map in so many silos. Attempts to rein in practice by tightening supervision or by prescribing instructional solutions either lead to resistance or to superficial compliance. By contrast, we have seen in Garden Grove that focus is a process of interrelated forces at work. Garden Grove starts with a vision of quality instruction and pursues it by building the individual and collective capacity of teachers and administrators to do the work that best gets results. The district then reinforces this through the teachers and administrators they hire and develop on the job, who assess how well students are faring on indicators of performance, while self-correcting as they go.

We also see in highly effective leaders that they build an ever-expanding guiding coalition of leaders who have a common focus about goals and about strategy (how to get there). It starts with the senior team—in Garden Grove's case, the superintendent and the half dozen other central office staff—and extends to school principals and coaches such as the forty-seven teachers on special assignment who work with individual schools. In this way, leaders stay the course and are not easily distracted from the core agenda. It is no accident that the new superintendent, Gabriela Mafi, is coming from within the culture having been Laura Schwalm's superintendent of secondary school instruction.

Focus does not mean more of the same; it is a process quality more than a content quality. Thus, it can serve continuous improvement as well as innovation that will be necessary in more uncertain times that may arise in the coming years. The Common Core State Standards, local funding and accountability in California's new laws, digital ubiquity, students' socioemotional needs, and much more may contribute to this uncertainty.

Sanger Unified

Located in California's Central Valley, Sanger Unified is about a quarter of the size of Garden Grove with 10,800 students and twenty schools. The demographics are similar: 73 percent low income and 84 percent minority (mostly Latino with a growing group of Asians). In 1999, the local union took out a billboard advertisement that declared, "Welcome to the home of four hundred unhappy teachers." In 2004, it was named as one of the ninety-eight (out of 1,009) lowest-performance districts in the state and put on notice as a program-improvement district (David & Talbert, 2013).

By 2014, less than a decade later, Sanger students outpaced the state performance for English learners on the state's academic performance index (API)—770 versus 718. On the overall state index in which a score of 800 is the state goal, Sanger rapidly moved up to 820 compared to a state average of 788. A union leader observed that "there is not one principal in this town I would not work for" (David & Talbert, 2013, p. 3). How did Sanger do it?

Marc Johnson was appointed superintendent in 2004 and set the tone by saying to school principals that being on the watch-list was a wake-up call they could use to their benefit. The story is similar, in essence, to Garden Grove's. Once again, success boils down to persistent focus on a small number of key interrelated elements. Jane David and Joan Talbert (2013) note, "District leaders have stuck to a vision of what their learning organization would look like and a few principles for moving the system in that direction" (p. 5).

David and Talbert (2013, p. 8) identify three key principles that underpinned the Sanger Unified journey.

1. Take a developmental approach to change. (Change takes time; select a few complementary strategies, and stay focused year after year.)

2. Ground decisions in evidence. (Look closely at student data to define priorities, use feedback loops to test out and improve approaches, and use evidence to identify and spread effective practices.)

3. Build shared commitments and relationships to sustain change. (Communicate purpose, build trust, and foster ownership around effective practices.)

As with Garden Grove, what we see in Sanger Unified is a combination of an intense commitment to the moral imperative that all students can learn and a tight focus on execution through building relationships in order to get results. David and Talbert (2013, p. 7) pinpoint the shift in district culture in four dimensions:

1. From professional isolation to collaboration and shared responsibility

2. From following the textbook to diagnosing student learning needs

3. From principals as managers to principals as leaders of adult learning

4. From top-down mandates and compliance to reciprocal accountability

The Sanger Unified case is also instructive about how effective accountability works. There is a deep student-centered commitment to a nonpunitive climate (data are used to focus on improvement) and transparent results and practice that serve to leverage further improvement. Schools are held accountable for using evidence for more than literal results (of course using evidence contributes to better, more valid results). The district holds itself accountable for providing principals and schools with what they need to become successful. This reciprocal accountability is the bond we also saw in Garden Grove (central office service mentality in exchange for high expectations that performance will increase in quality and impact). Progress is continually reviewed in an open climate with corrective action built in.

Leadership Encore

We can now relate more explicitly what we have seen in Garden Grove and Sanger Unified to the leadership qualities and competencies we have discussed in previous chapters. We interviewed Laura Schwalm in July 2013 and asked what she has learned about effective leadership. She commented that more important than knowledge, intelligence, and commitment is "the ability to execute—to get things done." Such leaders invest in the time to understand individuals and group dynamics. Leaders, Laura offers, are good team players as well as good team leaders. They are good at building effective teams. They have the courage to do the right thing even if it is not popular. They do not comply for the sake of compliance but act for the sake of influencing learning. Because they know how to get buy-in for the terms of accountability, they are perceived as fair even when they are firm.

Laura goes on to say (reinforcing our main point in chapter 4 and this chapter about *focus*) that:

> Leaders are extremely self-disciplined. They set a few very clear, specific and often ambitious goals. They are patiently persistent. . . . Ultimately they have a powerful compass that helps them gain their equilibrium when the inevitable failures and disappointments arise, which provides them with the resiliency necessary for effective leadership. (L. Schwalm, personal communication, July 2013)

Sensitive that there is a lot of push in effective leaders' behavior, Laura is also alert to the balance of push and pull. Leaders develop a keen sense of when to lead and when to follow. As she puts it, "Highly effective leaders are often rather humble individuals who prefer to keep a low profile while keeping the spotlight on the work and those who are doing it" (personal communication, July 2013). Above all, these leaders "combine high and relentless focus with excellent peripheral vision" about what is going right and what might be problematic (personal communication, July 2013).

We can conclude this chapter by returning to how the seven competencies work in combination, keeping in mind what Laura Schwalm, Marc Johnson, and their leaders did to accomplish amazing results under very challenging circumstances.

Both of these leaders were willing and even compelled to challenge the status quo and do the right thing for their students. With their clear sense of direction and persistence, they were both able to challenge assumptions that were blocking student learning and stay the course to reach the results that were imperative. Each leader set clear expectations from day one. The trust from all constituents built over time because he or she followed through on his or her proposed actions with relentless precision. These leaders communicated regularly with all parties who needed to be on board.

They each had a commonly owned plan that was clear and concise and not riddled with countless mandates and initiatives that would distract their team. They continually reviewed their plan and tracked and communicated their progress. These two leaders were all about team over self. Their ability to be humble and still build the credibility of their vision to align all parties to their goals was inspirational. They both focused on relationships as the key to gaining support for change and maintaining the drive to sustainability.

Each environment was steeped with continuous improvement. Data were used to inform the work, not to blame people for failure. These leaders wanted everyone around them to improve, and they put their time into developing leaders.

The sense of urgency for change and improvement was an internal aspect for both leaders, aided at times by the pressure from external forces. However, both leaders wanted the results to be sustainable by building true learning environments within which people became self-motivated for change and continuous improvement. While not outlined in this chapter, both leaders formed countless partnerships and alliances with community groups and key public officials to pave the way for the changes and improvements needed for success.

It is important to note that while these leaders modeled the seven competencies every day in their work, there are a few cautions to consider when building and sustaining results-oriented districts and schools. As Laura Schwalm states, discipline is a key to sound implementation. Vision without execution will not be realized over time. Results-oriented environments must be able to move quickly and clearly to the core of what is both enabling results to occur and identifying areas that block progress. Too much focus on process and relationships could get in the way of the direct, honest discussions that must occur in districts and the ability to prevent being bogged down in too much process. In addition, leaders who focus too much on internal change can become susceptible to missing the opportunities to communicate in a timely manner to outside groups in the community. To sustain change, remember that we must bring along outside partners, such as municipal government, to the plans for success.

The bottom line is that the leaders in Garden Grove and Sanger Unified exemplified the seven competencies and built capacity and ownership across the district. Together, staff within the district got results. Capacity, ownership, and results create a recipe for sustainability.

One of the great advantages of districts that focus and start to get better and better results is that they are great places to work. They attract people who want to make a difference. Good people attracting and working with other good people get even better. Districts that have moved from compliance to focus tend to have a "come work with us" quality about them.

Having a "Come Work With Us" Quality

If you build it, they will come. Most of us remember the movie *Field of Dreams* about creating dreams that seem impossible, but if you believe, they can become a reality. While schools and districts are not Hollywood, they can be a place for dreams and hopes for students and families. And when dreams start to become reality, people in your district will notice, and word will spread about your successes. Pretty soon, your good staff members will want to stay, and talented new people will want to come and work in your district.

Leading with the seven leadership competencies turns dreams and hopes into reality for your teachers and administrators. Attracting the best talent and cultivating the people you already have as leaders are crucial for success in the modern educational climate. Just remember that if you do not attract and develop the best, the top people will leave. They can get a job somewhere else and usually at a higher salary. The average and low performers will stay and create difficulty for students and staff as you try to meet very challenging goals every day.

It is important to know that most talented people are looking for a reason to stay, not a reason to leave. If they see themselves as part of a vibrant, challenging, productive learning environment, they will stay and bring their friends. As recruiters always say, if you want to find a talented person, ask your best performer for a recommendation. The talented people move in flocks, and, unfortunately, the same can be said for low performers.

Make Life Easier

Can you imagine getting up every morning looking forward to coming to work, greeting your students, and seeing all your colleagues? You feel safe and energized in your work environment because you know that everyone you work with wants you to succeed and is willing to help you in any way possible. When you go home, at a reasonable time, you are not tired and stressed, so you can be present and focused for your family. When you spend time with friends, you tell them about your day or week and feel confident that you are making a difference in students' lives. Your friends feel your positive energy and want to learn about opportunities to work in the district. You feel proud at work and are active every day in challenging, rewarding work, but you have time to think, to be strategic, and to break the vicious cycle of just reacting to every problem each day.

I know it seems that we are back in Hollywood or maybe in Fantasyland at Disneyland. We must create these environments for students and staff to be able to create the energy needed for a learning environment steeped in innovation and to get the results we all want for our students. The evidence is clear—the successful districts and superintendents that we have cited in the previous chapters have developed district cultures where good people develop and want to stay. They love their work and their peers because together they are accomplishing amazing things for and with their students and communities.

Hire a Capacity Leader as Your Superintendent

We must be honest—no school system is nirvana; we all have difficult days, stressful situations, angry parents, budget constraints, and worries about safety. However, we are at a crucial time in education where the natural forces of accountability and compliance are creating environments filled with stress, fear, caution, and people wanting to leave the profession. So many teachers and administrators count their days to retirement. Talented people who had an interest in education are choosing other fields because they see education as an industry with no real opportunities to enjoy the work of helping students succeed. We will know the tide is turning when the most-attended workshops at administrator conferences are no longer those discussing retirement benefits and formulas.

So you want to know how to meet this challenge and begin to change your schools and districts into exciting, energized places to work that attract the best talent? Here's how.

Step one is to find the best leaders. There is research from many studies, such as the Wallace Foundation (2010), that finding the best teachers is the number-one factor in improving student achievement and that the best principal is the number-two factor for success. The definition of *best principal* is a key theme for us to ensure that we focus on sustainable improvements. Note, however, that we said in chapter 1 that it is not sufficient to search for the best *individuals*. You must build cultures of people working together. It is the social and decision capital of the group that powers individual development and collective efficacy.

We need to expand our vision of leadership to the right superintendent and central administrators to develop creative, enjoyable learning environments. In addition, we need to include the school board and the union leadership, if applicable, to our definition of *leadership*. Most research on leadership focuses on the principal. However, the superintendent sets the tone for the district. While the superintendent cannot do it alone, he or she must be able to develop a strong leadership cadre throughout the district and at the same time engage the school board in its critical role in creating a positive environment for everyone. In essence, we see this central leadership as constituting a kind of informal guiding coalition that interacts around goals and strategies that develop the kind of consistency of message and focus of work that we see in Garden Grove and Sanger Unified. Too often an energized, visionary superintendent is hired to create change and bring a district to success and finds him- or herself losing energy, getting mired in politics, or getting stuck in the office dealing with accountability pressures from the state and federal government.

We need to change our focus from the principal to the superintendent (and then back to the principal) to create sustainable change. A superintendent who knows how to create system change and motivate his or her team to the highest results and bring back the joy of learning for everyone is rare but not extinct. In short, to create sustainable improvements we need to hire and develop capacity builders as our leaders—capacity leaders.

Capacity leaders know how to create sustainable change and find and develop leaders who can maintain the modern culture. Capacity leaders are committed to their districts—to distributing leadership and ensuring that there is a culture of empowerment that can be results focused. The added skill is the ability to partner with the school board in the leadership and change efforts. The superintendent must have the skills to work closely with the board to lead together while creating the space and freedom for him to lead the district. The ability to shift the board to a strategic role focusing on the community and external environment is not easy for most superintendents.

Another problematic scenario occurs when a strong superintendent is determined to take the reins of the district and expects the board to allow him or her to lead without micromanaging. Then, the board begins to move into an operational role and the superintendent feels threatened and either fights back for his or her territory or gives in and loses control over creating the culture of excellence he or she must be able to establish. Unfortunately, the road is lined with many superintendents who have fallen into the trap of fight or flight. Many of these superintendents leave early or are not renewed for a second contract.

This instability in districts is often influenced by good principals and administrators leaving for greener pastures. While we agree that we must have the best teachers and principals to improve student achievement, we need to have a superintendent who can keep his or her job and have time to create a capacity for sustainable improvements. The capacity leader knows that leadership has to be broad in the district, from the school board to teacher leaders, in order to maintain success well beyond his or her tenure.

Build a Team of Capacity Leaders

The capacity leader superintendent recognizes that he or she must challenge the status quo (the first competency) to hire the best. Superintendents must free up time to be the number-one recruiter in the district. They must be relentless in looking for talent at conferences, meetings, and in conversations with their colleagues and community leaders. Depending on the size and complexity of their districts, they should also take advantage of recruiters who can increase their pool of talent, especially for positions that are difficult to attract with the best. Most superintendents realize that hiring a special education director or business manager may be even harder than hiring a great principal. These positions can be critical in both service delivery and finances and could make or break the superintendency.

The best superintendents also realize that while tradition in education involves setting up very inclusive hiring processes to increase parent or key constituent ownership for a new hire, too much process can be a problem. One superintendent of a high-performing district believed that he must honor the tradition of letting the broad-based search committee select the final three candidates for him to hire. The problem was that the superintendent recruited a candidate who he believed was perfect for assistant superintendent of curriculum and instruction. Unfortunately, the search committee did not recommend the superintendent's recruit. The superintendent, who was not willing to challenge the status quo, hired a new assistant superintendent and let his candidate go to another district. The person he hired was adequate but not excellent.

A superintendent of a large urban district in the Midwest wanted to hire a new director of student services and believed that she did not have any candidates internally who would be excellent. She recognized that she could not find the best candidate alone and asked a recruiter for assistance. The board would not allocate the $5,000 to hire the external consultant, so the superintendent ended up hiring an internal candidate who did not really want the job and was less than adequate.

As the superintendent finds his or her group of leaders, he or she must put the time and sustained energy into building a high-performance team. This involves working with each administrator on his or her own leadership development. This can be accomplished by completing leadership assessments (Kirtman, 2014), assessing emotional intelligence, and completing 360-degree review processes. We need to only hire leaders who are willing to be vulnerable and look at their strengths and weaknesses and engage in continual learning (competency six—"has a commitment to continuous improvement for self and organization"). Their ego must be strong but not too dominating. They must be able to bring out and listen to the voices around them. The superintendent must model the personal leadership development process and only hire leaders who will engage in a similar effort for personal development. Leaders must be able to model the personal leadership process by sharing their leadership profiles with their teams.

Scott Kuffel, superintendent in Geneseo, Illinois, a small rural district, is committed to his learning and development and models this behavior for his team. His team has a norm called *straight talk*. This means that people need to be direct and honest in meetings and in their work in schools and the district. If a team member feels someone is playing games and not being honest, he or she can call out this behavior in either a team meeting or privately. He cites numerous occasions that his administrators have asked him for a private meeting to give him feedback when they believe he is not demonstrating straight talk. He also explained that, prior to one meeting, one of his principals received straight talk from a colleague on behavior that was not conducive to building trust. The principal called a special meeting of the other principals and took responsibility for his behavior and apologized for his actions (S. Kuffel, personal communication, August 5, 2014).

The superintendent is creating an environment in which straight talk occurs regularly without any repercussions. This continuous learning and personal accountability system has resulted in significant change in a very conservative district that has improved student achievement. It is important to build a leadership team in which everyone is trying to help his or her colleagues be successful. One department of education administrator felt frustrated by the continuous silos and competitiveness among her colleagues. People held back information that could be helpful to others to gain approval from their supervisors at the expense of others. This lack of teamwork created a competitive environment that was not seen as a service center to help districts succeed. The administrator left the department of education and found a job at an education foundation. Now, she feels excited about her work and her colleagues and believes they support each other and share in the accomplishments of the entire organization.

Another district has a capacity-building superintendent who is committed to learning and modeling behavior that creates energy and excitement. However, an assistant superintendent models punitive behavior to the principals and encourages a fear-based culture. While the district is improving, this central administrator's behavior is clearly holding it back from success. In fact, there seems to be a good cop / bad cop phenomenon in some urban districts (in which Lyle has worked) that are under pressure to focus on account-ability and compliance.

The superintendent is the good cop trying to inspire true leader-ship. However, to handle the pressures of accountability, the district hires a bad cop administrator to enforce the requirements of man-dates and rules established on the federal, state, and local levels. Hiring workhorses to monitor compliance is seen as necessary for the 21st century world of education. However, these designated or self-appointed compliance officers create a toxic environment in these districts. The messages of positive feedback, motivation, and innovation are countered with fear, blame, and hesitancy in leaders. In short, bad cops are only good for compliance; good cops motivate people to do better.

It is important for our capacity-leader superintendents to make sure that the message is consistent and motivation and results ori-ented. We must not have a subculture of fear that kills the joy of success. This does not mean that people can do whatever they want and not feel accountable. In fact, the seven competencies together produce greater de facto accountability than any punitive surveil-lance system can ever accomplish.

The capacity leader builds a culture where people want success for all students and can have honest, direct discussions and feedback for performance that is critical and positive. Evaluations are still there to remove the poor performers. While it is true that the best performers can survive and even accomplish good results despite the toxic envi-ronment, the majority of people will withdraw from the fear-based subculture. In a good culture, top performers do even better and contribute to the betterment of their colleagues.

In one district, the superintendent has been building his dream team and has worked relentlessly on capacity building of leaders and is training and developing aspiring leaders. However, one of his central office leaders has created a subculture of fear. This leader is talented but mistreats people. The superintendent is unaware of how this particular leader is affecting his goals. This is why all leaders on the team must be engaged in their own growth and development. The central office leader creating the subculture of fear has turned down coaching opportunities, which is a sign of a leader who is not open to continuous improvement (competency six). Thus, his boss, the superintendent, needs to look beyond individual talent to determine the impact on the wider group, which in this case, is fostering a toxic environment. An individual, isolated high performer, as many sports teams have discovered, can be a negative asset.

Unleash the Power of Teacher Leaders

We must unleash the power of teacher leaders; they are our real instructional leaders. At one conference we attended, a teacher from a large urban district stood up and said that principals are too stretched to be real instructional leaders. She said a quick observation or fast feedback in the hall is not helpful to a teacher's development. She continued by saying that principals are not very visible in the school, often being tied up in meetings and in their office with paperwork. In fact, another teacher told a story of her principal who was so busy when trying to observe her class that the principal ended up mistakenly handing the teacher notes for improvement that pertained to another teacher. She said she felt sorry for her principal but was very frustrated herself. Michael (Fullan, 2014) has documented a growing *micromanagement madness* from principals that is detrimental to the school developing an instructionally oriented culture that becomes effective at schoolwide student achievement. Principals need to build their teacher leaders into a team that can be helpful for the school. While some districts are saying they want the principal to be the instructional leader, it is not realistic or even advisable. We do want principals to be pedagogically knowledgeable, not to work with each teacher one by one, but rather to help lead the group. We want principals to reduce initiatives, simplify plans, and decrease their time spent on compliance. This will allow principals to be visible in their schools and to have the time to build the leadership capacity of the teachers. Successful schools have a culture where peers can give feedback to each other on best practices and areas for improvement.

Principals need to spend their time on high-impact strategy discussions with their teams. Some instructional leadership teams at the school level do not understand what it means to be a leadership team. One leadership team in an underperforming school stated that it thought its job was to just listen to the state assistance people about what to do and give some feedback. Due to fear, honest feedback was missing.

Now, the school is learning about what a real teacher leadership team can do to help the principal and assistant principal improve results. It identified culture issues that were blocking progress: veteran teachers refusing to help new teachers, lack of principal availability, poor communication, and a negative school self-image. This new energized leadership team has explored its leadership style and has engaged in self-improvement work. The results are already paying off. One of the best teachers in the school who had a low score on a leadership assessment for initiative has begun to step up and lead improvement efforts in mathematics. Now that she is showing more leadership, she is encouraging other teachers to join her in improvement efforts.

Create the Buzz of Success

Remember the fun and joy we want in our schools and districts? When leaders and teams are in place, we must begin to infuse positive energy. Leaders who show positive energy often create positive environments. While there are data showing that extroverts often have an easier time creating excitement, introverts can also be successful (Kirtman, 2014). Fun events, cheerleading, and public encouragement motivate some people. More personal, private conversations and true reflective learning motivate others. A district leadership team and a school team can develop a plan with the right mix for its culture.

Sue Szachowicz, a successful principal in Brockton, Massachusetts, with 4,200 students in a very diverse district, created a feeling of pride for everyone. She hung banners outside and inside her school showing accomplishments, created a video to show its culture of excellence for students, and went on the road nationally to tell the school's story. The pride in the school was contagious, and the staff felt ownership and pride for their accomplishments. While Sue was a major extrovert and inspirational speaker, she always led with the students first.

Another principal in a large urban district in the Midwest was more introverted and was not creating the energy he needed for success. Once he saw the leadership profile of his team, he realized he was more of a behind-the-scenes implementer. He noted that he had highly energetic and influence-oriented leaders on his team. However, he did realize that they felt held back by his style and were withdrawing from any leadership role in the school. As a good implementer, he coached these potential leaders to help him create the positive energy and buzz of excitement in the school. The teacher leaders were very excited that the principal asked them to help when they felt their style was previously not being recognized. They helped him create a culture where staff wanted to be in the school and prove to the district that they could be successful. This school became one of the highest performing in the district.

We need to encourage principals to take risks and create these positive environments for innovation. In order to help principals, superintendents and central office administrators need to be supportive and helpful. They cannot discourage risk taking and creativity. It is also important for the school board and the community to support the principal's efforts. The school board can generate this support by promoting the goals and practices it wants to see from leaders to the community and especially by hiring superintendents who model these traits.

An example of this can be seen in Mississippi, where the seven competencies are incorporated in the community- and parent-engagement trainings. This is one of the program offerings from the National Institute for School Leadership program (NISL), a statewide instructional leadership program. Using the seven competencies to develop strategies for community and parent involvement will align districts' internal and external leadership work throughout the state. This coherence between all levels of leadership both internally and externally is very important for positive change. Too many principals have had complaints from parents, teachers, and community members for being out of the district during important conferences on key areas like the Common Core, school culture, and data analysis and assessment. It is important for stakeholders to see a principal forming new partnerships in the community and to be congratulated for his or her work. Too often people might see a principal out of the building and complain that he or she should be in the school.

One superintendent who is very focused on results and has been able to lead schools to higher test scores received a poor review from the teachers about morale in the district. While results are important and need to be celebrated, morale can be poor in districts that are not creating positive work environments. Next time her leadership team met, members implemented a new practice that began to change morale. Leadership team meetings were held at different schools each week. In each leadership team meeting, the superintendent asked staff in the school to drop in for breakfast, which was led by a different chef (senior team member) each week. The chefs established different themes, like Pancake Day, and cooked for anyone who stopped by.

While this gesture began to show that the leadership team was there to serve the staff, the team also set up a series of meetings with staff to learn about how senior team members could improve morale and create an enjoyable and productive work environment. The team realized from its leadership assessments that it was great at driving results at a fast pace but that team members' skills and behaviors about listening and building strategies with broader ownership were weak. They began to work on their skills at influencing and listening, which slowed down some of their initiatives but broadened their capacity for sustaining improvements.

Companies like Amazon and Google try to create fun events for staff. They even have ping-pong tables for employees to get a break and do something active. Districts are afraid to do this in schools or at a district level. One town office put in a wellness program and a gym in its basement for staff. It informed the community and started a fundraiser for grants and donations to support the program. Morale improved in the town almost immediately, as did the results of their work. The town departments involved services such as permits, recreation, finances, and other town services. School and districts can take similar actions with the right type of leadership and by bringing the community along.

Formalize the Program to Attract and Develop Talent

In industry, health care, and some public-sector organizations, leaders have realized that talent development is the competitive element for success. In industry, talent management is fast becoming one of the key areas for competitive advantage on par with innovation. Education, on the other hand, has not excelled in recruiting and building individual and collective talent.

As the focus in education has been almost exclusively on instructional leadership, another counter trend has emerged. The number and quality of candidates for teaching and administration have been dwindling consistently for years. So why is education so slow to catch up to the talent trend that has been the key to success for the private sector? "Advertise for positions, and they will come" has been an assumption for many years. When they do not come, we hire whoever is available and hope for the best. Somehow, we also believe that they will magically do a great job and learn and develop as educators.

Many positions are filled too quickly, and people settle for the best available candidate. In this scenario, personnel or human resource offices tend to make safe choices, often focusing on compliance and liability issues. We need instead to seek talent and build cultures where good people want to work with other good people.

Traditional personnel administrators are transactional in nature. They focus on job openings, advertisements, grievances, and personnel problems. Instead, education needs to hire leaders in talent management who are transformation-oriented. While the transaction functions still need to be followed, the transformational work needs to get much more attention. This involves workforce planning, looking at data for retirements and positions that are hard to fill with the best people. Each district needs a plan to determine its profile of teachers and leaders.

Then, a focus on recruitment needs to be developed. The term *sourcing* is used in the talent-management world. This simply means identifying where you find the best people and how you will attract them to apply. While the talent-management office can organize this effort, all the leaders need to look for talent. For smaller districts, this talent focus can be done without a lot of resources by increasing the focus and commitment to getting the best.

The practice of posting ads and hoping for the best is outdated. Most successful leaders recruit the best they can find. This means find people that fit your district's short- and long-term needs. Advertisements should not provide your main source of applicants—they should supplement your pool only. You want to know more about your candidates than you will find from normal applications. Do people you respect recommend them? Can you find the real story about them, not just read their letters of recommendation? We must also learn about who these people are, not just what they have done.

Guy Fincke, of Vistage, Inc., once said, "We hire people for what they have done and fire people for who they are." Just because a person has the right degrees and experience does not mean he or she can be a capacity builder as a leader. In fact, the highest technically skilled people often are not strong at developing people. Another key adage is to hire for attitude and train for skills.

We need to encourage superintendents and other leaders to recruit and find people and not be held back by traditional hiring practices that often support hiring people who make a diverse team happy and may not be able to create the change you want. John Antonucci, superintendent in Westwood, Massachusetts, talks to recruits personally to see if they are a good fit. In addition, he also sees his role as selling the district to talented people. He uses recruitment services, if necessary, and will not hire anyone to just fill a job. He would put in an interim person rather than settle. Recruiters have an established network of candidates for key positions. In addition, they identify high-performing people for key roles and check to see if they are interested in an open position. If they are not, the recruiter will ask them to recommend candidates. High performers tend to recommend other skilled leaders (J. Antonucci, personal communication, May 10, 2014).

Education has also been very slow in using leadership assessments as part of hiring. Many fields use inventories such as the DiSC, Workplace Personality Inventory, and other assessments to add to the hiring process. This allows the supervisor to have objective information on a candidate to weigh against other data used in the process.

Once the person is hired, it is advisable to do an entry plan to help the new person assess the situation and listen and learn from all the key constituencies (Jentz, 1982). This process builds ownership and support for potential change efforts. Once the entry plan is complete, the principal can build his or her leadership team and begin the capacity-building effort, which means identifying the team's areas for growth from day one and building on the strengths identified in the hiring process.

Now, we can tie the professional development and evaluation process to the talent-management program. Instead of evaluation being a separate process based on state rubrics, it should be an outgrowth of the hiring process. Goals can be developed based on the district's, school's, and department's needs. Then, we add in the results of the leadership assessments to form a leadership-development plan. The supervisor would engage in continuous feedback with the new hire on his or her plan and the new hire's leadership growth.

Professional development and coaching for the new person could be offered to help the talent blossom. Coaches should be trained on the district's goals and how to use leadership assessment to help each person hired reach his or her potential. The coaches need to learn how to give direct critical feedback to maximize learning. While they are there to support the leader, they have to be driven by results and outcomes.

A talent-management program is continuous and a focus for all supervisors. The leaders need to also understand that keeping talent means understanding fit. We want to hire someone because his or her competencies fit the needs of the district.

However, people's *fit factor* can change. We can define *fit* as the interests, skills, environment, opportunity, and work-life balance. If someone has the skills for the role but is not interested in the new job, he or she will lose interest or become ineffective. If someone states his or her interest and has the appropriate skills, but there are no opportunities, then he or she will lose motivation. The environment the person works in is also important and can change. Some people want the challenge of a problem school; others like urban over suburban or small over large.

The good leader has continual conversations with his or her staff on the fit factor. Life changes can also affect fit. A great teacher suddenly has a change in family situation requiring a more flexible day. This lack of fit that did not exist originally is now causing stress. A principal needs to be aware of this early and see if any adjustments can be made to keep the fit factor high. This may seem like a lot of work. It isn't if you see finding and keeping talent as a key to success.

You cannot hire your way to good cultures any more than you can, as Linda Darling-Hammond so aptly says, fire your way to Finland (she was referring to the fact that Finland has great teachers, and some policymakers wanted to employ teacher evaluation as a weapon to fire weak teachers (L. Darling-Hammond, personal communication, 2014). People create good cultures, but they are also attracted to them. Talented schools (cultures) improve weak teachers. Talented teachers leave weak schools; just as they are attracted to talented cultures, where they tend to stay and contribute to the culture getting even better. It is a virtuous circle, indeed, where leaders hire talented teachers as part of the process of improving school cultures, and as these cultures get stronger, good teachers stay, and the more good teachers stay and add up, the more other talented teachers are drawn to work in these organizations.

Thus, "Come work with us" is not just a normal human resource issue. It is part of the interlocking development of a well-led collective culture that we have been describing. By working to make things simpler and focused, by moving compliance to the side in favor of capacity building, and by developing an attractive work culture for incumbents and others who want to join—and when they join, want to stay—the work becomes more effective and deeply satisfying.

Changing the Game—Anytime, Anywhere

If you can make it here, you can make it anywhere! These are words often heard in schools and districts across the United States, but they are not optimistic words. The words seem to be uttered wistfully as if no one can really be successful under our circumstances. Urban districts face enormous challenges with great diversity, extreme city politics, and pressure from the state and federal government on test scores. Rural districts believe that their challenges are unique based on the often large areas their districts cover, lack of resources with a low business tax base, difficulty attracting talent to move to their communities, and politics. They often feel like their state's forgotten and ignored child. Suburban districts believe they have challenges based on the number of entitled parents, politics (once again), unrealistic expectations, and lack of resources due to the state's focus on helping urban districts. Who is right that their job is more difficult?

They are all right. The challenges are daunting everywhere at times, but the best leaders can and have adjusted to leading in multiple geographical settings. If a leader is focused on capacity building, he or she finds and develops the best talent to lead the district while staying focused on student needs. The distractions are similar in each setting: too many initiatives, too much compliance, and too many distractions. Each setting challenges the leaders differently on the issues that we have discussed so far.

Leaders Transform Their Cultures

In the urban districts, the weight of the state requirements on accountability are immense and can suffocate the leader who is not strong or skilled at managing the onslaught of just one more initiative. Paul Dakin, superintendent in Revere, Massachusetts, has led his district to higher performance in all schools. In fact, Revere High School has been nationally recognized for its extraordinary improvement in student learning and achievement.

When Paul is asked how he prevents himself from falling into the reactive, compliance trap, he quickly states two guidelines that are always on his mind. He says, "I hire and support the most talented people I can find to put on my team." Paul is a strong leader who has a profile that focuses on results, not compliance. The second area, he says, is "I look at each task that comes across my desk and determine if it helps me with my long-term goals. If it does I act, if it does not I delegate the work and put less attention to it" (P. Dakin, personal communication, July 1, 2014).

Paul is now trying to build capacity in his district for sustained improvement. He is a true capacity builder who is committed to leadership development, professional development, and coaching for all his leaders. His high-performing high school has attracted significant funds from a foundation to help staff maintain their efforts.

Lorenzo Garcia, a principal in Paul's district, is a results-oriented leader who will be focusing on capacity building to maintain the gains already achieved.

Pedro Galaviz, superintendent of a small urban district in El Paso, Texas, has embraced the challenges as a new superintendent. His district has had very low expectations for student achievement. The professionalism that exists in high-performing districts has never been a priority for his community. Pedro has committed to capacity building and establishing the highest expectations for all students. He also is committed to coaching all his leaders to build teams and helping them become reflective learners. He continually models this behavior by discussing the latest research and how his leadership team's practice can change to meet students' diverse needs. Pedro also realizes he needs to invest in his school board's leadership development to ensure that members are partners in the long road ahead for excellence.

Brett Kustigian, superintendent of a small rural district we discussed in chapter 4, thinks as if he has unlimited resources to provide all students with the highest level of education. He knows he has to form partnerships with universities, businesses, consultants, and any possible resource to supplement his small budget. He hired a full-time development person to obtain grants to add to his resource base. He openly states that he wants his district to be the most innovative district in America. He has made all three schools innovation schools, which is a classification from the secretary of education in Massachusetts. His district is the only one that has all schools designated as innovation schools.

Karen Rue, superintendent in a Texas suburban environment, has been a transformational leader since day one of her tenure. She has partnerships with businesses, universities, and public and private organizations to enhance the services for her students. She continually invests in her team and staff for professional development on leadership. Next, she will be working on leadership development for her school board. Her test scores for student achievement are exemplary, and her district's success story is extraordinary. She is never satisfied with her district's accomplishments and always looks for improvement opportunities. She has demanding parents whom she greets and listens to with an extraordinary customer service ability. She has a full-time community relations person who focuses on maintaining partnerships and meeting community needs. When she confronted severe budget cuts in Texas, she immediately rallied the community to support her district through the tight times.

Can These Leaders Be Successful in Different Settings?

Let's begin to look at what is common among these leaders. They are all confident and secure in their own ability to be successful. They are all innovative and open to new ideas. Each one forms partnerships with multiple parties, both public and private. They are all focused more on results than compliance and do not let the day-to-day distractions take them off course.

Each one has strong networking skills and is obsessed with capacity building and sustaining the results he or she has achieved. They are engaging leaders who present well, can articulate a vision for their district, and can listen to other viewpoints. They have strong egos but do not let their egos get in the way of sustainable success. They think system first and have a long-term focus. Each one is willing to look at how he or she can improve every day as a leader and is not defensive about critical feedback. The communities are benefiting from each leader's success. They exhibit strengths on each of the seven competencies. What is more important is that they know their work on self-improvement is never done. They are and always will be continual learners.

Do the Same Qualities Work for Principals?

Susan Ambrozavitch is a high school principal in Danvers, Massachusetts. She moved from being a very successful elementary principal to leading a high school. She is a strong capacity builder and visionary leader. Her leadership profile shows an extreme focus on results and ability to look at her strengths and weaknesses openly with her staff and a commitment to every student's success.

Susan has taken on an assistant superintendent role while keeping her high school principal position. The district has benefitted from her vision, community relations skills, and results orientation. She could only do this work if she built leadership capacity in the high school. In 2013, Susan faced a terrible crisis in her school that received national news coverage. She used her passion for people around her and the support from the high school and throughout the district to handle this extraordinary pressure. By the way, Susan worked in the investment banking industry before she pursued her career in education. The fact that she has a broader set of skills from the private sector enhances her skills for the role in her district.

Allan Cameron, elementary principal and new superintendent in Wrentham, Massachusetts, is a true capacity-building leader. Allan had a successful military career and coaching from a strong superintendent, John Antonucci, to guide his leadership. John was a business manager and dispels the assumption that only an instructional leader can improve student achievement. Allan has been very innovative throughout his career. He is open to critical feedback from teachers and parents on his leadership to constantly improve. Allan was able to create an environment of continuous improvement in his school that resulted in the highest test scores in his state.

These principals have had careers that have allowed them to move up quickly because of their strong leadership skills. In some cases, they have worked at multiple levels in districts and have been able to transform cultures for their schools.

What do they have in common? They are innovative and always open to new ideas that can come from their community, colleagues, or other partners. They are very open and clear about their strengths and weaknesses and listen to critical feedback to improve. They want to get better at their craft every day. They are once again all low in compliance and rule following in the leadership assessments they completed for their development. They get results for students in every role they take. They all see improvement as a never-ending journey. They are, in short, continuous learners, which they model in their interaction with others.

It's revealing that the principals are very similar to the superintendents. They are all leaders who see their role as making everyone around them better. They are all building capacity to sustain gains for the long run and in some cases have moved to other districts and have demonstrated that the success continued after they left. They all have embraced the seven competencies and use them for their improvement and to build leadership in their schools. They use the right drivers and put very little time into the wrong drivers despite pressure around them to conform.

Why Doesn't Fear Stop the Best Leaders?

As Franklin D. Roosevelt stated, "The only thing we have to fear is fear itself." This age-old adage applies once again to the leaders we need in the 21st century. These leaders who build capacity do not let fear stop them. Fear can come from several factors. One fear that derails many leaders is feeling they will get in trouble if they do not comply with authority figures. While we could examine where this fear comes from in people and how those emotions were formed in their life, we will not take that path in this book. The confidence that a leader has comes from following his or her values and the knowledge that he or she is not breaking laws or being unethical. This allows them to pursue results for students. Paradoxically, leaders who exemplify the seven competencies, and thus take risks when they need to, not only do not get into trouble but actually *gain greater respect*.

One group of superintendents attended a statewide conference and heard more regulations and requirements to add to its plate from "The Commissioner" (state superintendent). The leaders reacted by assuming that they better do what they were being told or they would get in trouble. Other superintendents at the same conference directly expressed their concerns with these new mandates as not being value added and distracting from the work they needed to do in their districts. The fear-based leaders, reverting back to a childhood response, believed that they were going to get into trouble. They were succumbing to fear that would prevent them from staying the course to results.

As Dan Heath (2004), coauthor of *Switch: How to Change Things When Change Is Hard* (Heath & Heath, 2010), notes, change is primarily an emotional issue and cannot be effectively managed with just logic, information, and facts. Fear is perhaps the most primitive emotional response that humans have. Fear-prone leaders react as if they are going to get in trouble, while other leaders do not have the same emotional response. The logic says that the superintendents report to the school boards, not the state superintendent. While the superintendents who were fear prone could believe that state money could be taken away if they did not comply, the reality is that their fear was more emotional than factual.

More than that, leaders who lead *do* get in trouble sometimes, but they manage it because they have a lot of professional and local political confidence. Leaders sometimes believe that they could lose their job if they take a risk. If one is a real capacity leader, all constituents become part of the transformation process, which means that they would be less likely to interfere or ultimately fire the leader who was either innovative or bold in their actions. Correspondingly, these constituents would be more likely to protect the leader if higher authorities threaten him or her. Additionally, they have a trump card up their sleeves: the leaders cited in this book are frequently recruited for other positions and have great job security. Courageous but effective leaders will always have multiple opportunities.

Another fear factor lower-performing leaders often exhibit is the concern about overstepping boundaries and doing something now that could wait for someone else or the next leader to pursue. One principal candidate recounted this story. In her interview with the superintendent, she was told of some key issues that she needed to address that the current superintendent would delay. In mentioning this, the principal noted, why rock the boat now when he (the superintendent) could leave the issue for the next superintendent? The candidate decided to turn down the position because she was concerned that if the district lacked the leadership necessary to be successful, she did not want to join the team.

The best leaders do not fear that it may not be the right time for change and improvement nor do they leave the problem for the next person or worry if the board will agree. The most effective leaders create a sense of camaraderie and excitement for going beyond the minimum. They motivate all constituents to be part of the change effort and train them to handle everyone's concerns.

It is important to note that effective leaders do compromise, not based on fear but based on carefully listening to a variety of viewpoints and making sure that resources are allocated properly to get the best results. They are also holding up district values to keep everyone honest on what is right for the students. They might compromise based on managing the work environment for the staff and making sure staff are not too overwhelmed by change. Even when they do back off, it is through open dialogue with key people about the impact of actions on results, not due to emotional fear. Another characteristic of effective leaders is that they listen and adjust their thinking and actions in the light of new information and ideas.

Thus, the good news is that leaders who take appropriate actions— who do act according to the seven competencies—build a strong *political constituency* that gives them a powerful and positive political base. The seven competencies act as concerted relationship builders that give leaders greater power and influence.

Leaders Focus Through Good Times and Bad

The best leaders do not let the external conditions stop them from their focus on results. Too many leaders pull back on key transformational culture work during tight financial times. However, our best leaders maintain their focus despite budget problems.

Yes, resources are important for results. However, when building a strategy for sustainable improvement, one must factor in good and bad times. This requires strong financial planning and a clear focus on return on investment for all initiatives. If a leader is clear about how strategies designed toward meeting goals impact results, he or she can make informed choices.

Too often district leaders are so busy and reactive that they just implement initiatives that they think will impact results. They do not take the time to determine how they will know a strategy or new program will get results. Therefore, they waste scarce resources on programs that are popular or traditional but have low impact.

Leaders send their people to professional development programs and hope they make an impact. They often do not take time to really evaluate the program to make sure that it will have impact. The person who attends the professional development program should be coming back to train others if schools are to obtain the full benefit from the new knowledge.

An example of this is in the district's full investment in instructional coaching. The district hires strong instructional people and assumes they know how to coach teachers for better results. The emphasis on instruction often limits our understanding that coaching is a skill and an art and the best content people are not necessarily the best coaches. One instructional coach speaking about her role as a coach said, "I give the teachers the websites and books they need to read, and they should be able to use this knowledge to improve their teaching."

Unfortunately, this instructional coach does not understand coaching. She never was trained as a coach. To help a teacher learn new practices, the coach needs to be able to spend time building a relationship with his or her coachees. Coaches need to understand how the teachers feel about change and the new expectations that they are expected to meet. The coach should explore the best method to help the teacher learn and not just assume that the way he or she learns will work for the teacher. The coach also needs to support the teacher throughout the learning and change process.

This coach was never trained and the people aspect of the work—beyond content—was never discussed. The district assumed that content was enough and ignored the change and personal aspect of improvement. Therefore, the district is wasting the resources that it has been allocated for instructional improvement. The change process involves integrating both content and relationships.

In this case, the district is considering discontinuing the instructional coaching work due to budget constraints. This is a poor decision based on a cursory review of the problem and a lack of understanding about how to achieve sustainable results. It does not realize that properly selecting and training instructional coaches might have a major positive effect on student achievement.

Too often budget rules the day, and cuts are made equally across the board. If the budget needs to be reduced, there are two leadership concepts that need to prevail. First, have we established the added value of our strategies to meet the goals? A leader must be able to show how results will be improved through the effective use of resources. As illustrated in *Leadership and Teams*, most educational leaders are low in focus on return on investment (Kirtman, 2014). This means that most educators do not focus on how they know the funds are getting results. The approach to a finance committee or a mayor that we must have more money for students because they are our future will not work in gaining sustainable resources. People who do focus on dollars for impact want to see more analysis.

Second, the higher-performing leaders who are not mired in reactive, low-impact work also respond to bad times by using their broad-based relationships to bring in new revenue and support. The leaders who do not create transformative cultures spend all their time cutting resources. This kills morale and the spirit for success.

A leader of a special education consortium that provides services for thirteen districts knew how to build a network of support. When faced with severe budget constraints, he organized an event for key leaders statewide to celebrate the work of his collaborative (a consortium of thirteen school districts that share services in areas such as special education and transportation) and the impact on students. He asked for donations from all the participants, including the parents. The superintendents who were on the board of the collaborative were horrified by his approach and his lack of reality that these struggling parents would give money to the organization. They believed that the cost to hold the event would result in very low attendance and a loss of funds for the collaborative. In addition, they feared that the board would look insensitive to the parents, and they feared their reputations would be tarnished. They decided to send two of the board members to attend the event and to handle this pending crisis and manage the politics. Over five hundred people attended the program, and the donations were over $100,000. The positive energy in the room was amazing. The parents were happy to donate for a program that helped their children and clearly demonstrated value. Legislators attended and were impressed by the work of the collaborative. The staff were energized and felt great about the impact of their work.

Leaders Form a Support Network

Whether you are a superintendent, principal, special education director, or teacher leader, it is critical that you focus more attention on competency seven—"builds external networks and partnerships." Educators are slow to engage in social networking, feeling they have no time or afraid that it will be inappropriate. Ironically, students are better at social networking (although it can have its downsides) than adults—better at the very social learning skills that schools should be developing in the 21st century.

The best leaders have a support network and engage in regular use of social media. It is time for all leaders to begin to network with other highly energized, innovative, and fearless educators who want to change their districts and schools to places of joy for all students and staff. Joy and results do coexist in high-performing districts. Leaders need to find each other and spend time learning from other high performers.

Where can you find the time to form these networks? Decrease your time on statewide meetings announcing new mandates, compliance requirements, and new low-value initiatives. Remember you still need to comply and learn what you need to do to meet minimum requirements. However, save your time for more important efforts. Unfortunately, many statewide associations are not high impact in their programs and are also time wasters. This is not their fault. They are caught between the world of doing what their department of education tells them to do and what their members want. Therefore, too much of their time is spent reviewing the new evaluation system and setting up retirement sessions with members who can't wait to stop the pain of going to work every day.

While most effective leaders say they get very little benefit out of their statewide meetings other than networking with colleagues, they still go to these countless daylong programs. We challenge you to form valuable new networks with likeminded leaders and spend the time with them that you save from not attending the perfunctory programs. It is magic when capacity-building leaders who are committed to bringing the energy and excitement back to our schools and transforming their cultures to gain sustainable results come together. Their desire to learn and listen to others provides reinforcement and new strategies for improvement.

The support and resource bonanza that is immediately apparent when these leaders join forces is extraordinary. Three high-performing leaders from different states came together on a conference panel. They spent time learning about each other as people, leaders, and parents. This bond translated into one of the three leaders inviting the others to her district on the other side of the country to repeat the panel discussion on leadership with her principals. She said,

"Maybe the energy we have can be passed on to my people. We could even bring our people together to learn and help each other."

We see this magic across the United States and world when great leaders connect. They unite in similar values, an openness to learn, and the desire to build others' capacity in all of their districts. Now is the time to make this new network happen. We can visit each other, get together at national conferences, and use technology to meet through WebEx or GoToMeeting.

One former superintendent, Bob Maguire, decided to network with districts in China. He used technology and his visits to China to expand his network. He even held virtual professional development sessions with teachers in China. Now in retirement, Bob is a vice president of a company that brings students from China and other countries to America. His networking paid off for his district and for him with a new career after retirement (B. McGuire, personal communication, April 10, 2014).

Beyond these individual interactions we are now witnessing, Michael is centrally involved in a new powerful strategy that involves schools and districts learning from each other. These networks are formal, focused, and committed to continuous learning for students and leaders. Michael (Fullan, 2014) calls these leaders *system players*. In chapter 8, we talk about Leadership from the Middle (LFtM) as a further example of purposeful networking. Leaders who develop competency seven thrive in this new environment.

Leaders Know Incremental Change Is Not Enough

It is time for leaders to make a fundamental change, or as Tim Waters, Robert Marzano, and Brian McNulty (2003) call it, *second-order change*. In the business world, companies that do not dramatically change for today's and tomorrow's challenges go out of business. Companies such as Polaroid and Digital Equipment

Corporation who were industry leaders for many years are not even known to young leaders today.

IBM could have been one of these companies that fell by the wayside, but its leadership realized that survival was not based on inventing new products but on changing culture. The culture was too internal and had to shift to be externally focused on customers. Amazon makes sure that no one forgets the customers by having an empty chair in the room for the customer in most meetings (Anders, 2012). This forces the focus of discussion to meet the customer's needs, not the employees' needs.

Can you imagine if district meetings had an empty chair for the student during meetings? Could we see joint ventures between districts combining resources on new high-impact programs? Would we see corporate leaders and educational leaders working on joint ventures as equals? Will we see teachers leading districtwide efforts with administrators in support roles? Can you imagine students leading reform efforts as high school seniors?

We must realize that students *can* teach us! New companies are being led by twenty-two-year-olds, so imagine what students can do at seventeen. On a visit to the Cambridge Innovation Center in Massachusetts, a leadership group from a district trying to learn about the practical use of 21st century skills encountered a seventeen-year-old student from another district. Someone asked him who he was and how he ended up spending time in the innovation center with six hundred of the most innovative companies. He stated that he just invented a new app for a major technology company and was working on some updates after school. By the way, the student, who we did not believe could teach us, made $250,000 a year in his after-school job.

Maybe we should bring in our students and listen, and seek out our graduates who are in the real world for insights on how we can change. Would people attend a statewide conference session with alumni in the workplace to help determine what strategies can be used to increase the value of education?

As we said in chapter 1, you are not alone. Increasingly, student leaders are operating on the same level as adult leaders. True leaders welcome these new resources. There are now enough leaders who are deeply dissatisfied with the status quo (including students) that it is much easier to find kindred spirits on your journey toward new possibilities. When enough of these new leaders connect and coalesce, they can change the game—anytime, anywhere.

Creating System Breakthroughs— You Are Needed

The leaders in this book are challenging the status quo in another more fundamental way. Not only are they pushing for change at their local levels, but they are also questioning how the system as a whole operates. In other words, they are attacking the wrong policy drivers that we discussed in chapter 1. They know that bureaucratic, carrot-and-stick accountability that uses rewards and punishment as motivators does not work. They realize the limits of going it solo. They appreciate technology but not as a driver. They eschew multiple initiatives that create overload and confusion. Additionally, they work on collaborative focus, specific solutions, transparent data, and explicit links to measurable outcomes. By investing in focused capacity building, they are developing *internal accountability* in which the group is accountable for its performance, *and* these leaders interface willingly and openly to the external state accountability system.

Stated another way, what is problematic at the macro level (wrong drivers) and what can be right at the local level (district and schools) are being addressed simultaneously. There are a growing number of leaders with the common agenda of achieving whole-system change, and this means that the possibility for system breakthrough is within our grasp. In chapter 1, we said, "You are not alone." Now we are saying, "You are needed."

This new work is not business as usual. We are saying you need freedom from the constraints of the wrong drivers, but more than that, we are talking about the opportunity and competencies needed to take advantage of what could be done without such constraints. It is beyond this book to address the content of innovations that leaders should tackle with these new competencies. We do know that radical new developments are needed partly because traditional schooling is boring for both students and teachers, and largely because 21st century skills are not being addressed in the current school system. Michael is involved in a worldwide network of over one thousand schools working in cluster to implement "new pedagogies for deep learning" (www.newpedagogies.com). The deep learning outcomes include collaboration, communication, creativity, critical thinking, character, and citizenship. New pedagogies consist of a learning partnership between and among teachers, students, and parents. New pedagogies linked to deeper learning outcomes need to be accelerated by integrating the power of digital resources. Pedagogy is the driver; digital is the accelerator. The Common Core State Standards movement is also a forum for innovation. We don't think the CCSS, per se, are the answer, but they are a serious effort to address deeper goals (standards), innovative assessment systems, and better teaching, therein also providing a great opportunity for innovation.

These necessary movements toward substantial innovations that will increase performance and results are now underway. The whole enterprise will be a flop if we do not develop leaders who have the seven competencies and who can develop other leaders with these qualities. We need two things: the right focus, which we call *Leadership from the Middle* (LFtM), and the seven competencies necessary for leading the middle.

Leadership From the Middle

Andy Hargreaves, Henry Braun, and their team (2012) first surfaced the term LFtM in their study of ten school districts in Ontario. The government had allocated $25 million to the province's directors' association (superintendents are called *directors* in Ontario) to oversee the strategy for integrating special education into the mainstream and for improving student achievement overall across the seventy-two school districts that constitute Ontario's public school system. Hargreaves and his group studied in depth a representative sample of ten districts.

What they found was that the so-called middle (in this definition the government is the center, the districts are the middle, and local schools and communities are the lower level) can be a major force for change. The middle, when it is focused and well led, can come up with insightful ideas, generate widespread buy-in, and create stronger accountability with transparent data and better results. The middle does not operate on its own. It still relates upward to policy priorities and performance requirements and downward in collaboration with its schools. When the middle gets stronger, members become *better partners* (across the middle and with other districts, as well as upward and downward). Think of it this way: we know that top-down change does not work (you can't control the complexities from the center), and bottom-up change fails (some schools move, others don't); therefore, the middle, if orchestrated, can form the coherence, drive, and glue for system breakthrough.

In *Professional Capital: Transforming Teaching in Every School*, Hargreaves and Fullan (2012) take this one step further and conclude that "if you want to change the group use the group to change the group" (pp. 8–9). We can think of the middle in two different applications. Within the district, the schools are the middle; within the state, the districts are the middle. In chapter 5, we saw in Sanger Unified and Garden Grove that the leaders at the center established a focus and stayed with it, building capacity within and across schools. The school principals—the middle if you like—were pivotal within their schools but also across schools as they influenced and helped each other. Michael and his team are involved in a massive LFtM strategy in California (see Fullan, 2014). With 1,009 districts and over seven million students, there is no way that the state can drive the change; it would be unlikely that any decentralized strategy would produce anything but uneven, unsustainable results. We are now part of a movement (and that is indeed the best term) where several clusters of districts have formed coalitions to work together for three or more years at a time on specific improvement goals, helping each other and reporting publicly on their results. Additional reinforcement of the direction—which must simultaneously address capacity building, focus, coherence, and performance, including accountability—is being built. These developments include the governor's overhaul of the funding formula (called Local Control Funding Formula), altering the state accountability framework, and mobilizing the Association of California School Administrators (with its 16,000 members) to play a lead role in developing leadership competencies among their members.

The good news is that LFtM is an instantly sticky concept. Leaders know the current system is not working (the wrong drivers again) and are attracted to an alternative whereby they can play a direct leadership role to really improve the system on a large scale. It doesn't matter where you are in the United States as a school or district leader—those who want to make a difference are ready to play a bigger, more influential role. The opportunity to lead within and beyond your boundaries is palpable. When Marc Johnson, Laura Schwalm, and those like them went through their journeys beginning in the early

2000s, they did so by and large as lone stars. There were not many kindred spirits around, so they stuck to their knitting. Since then, scores of leaders are attracted to becoming part of a larger movement so that they can both deeply improve their districts and learn from and contribute to improving other districts and the system as a whole.

For this to work, leaders will need skills, which brings us back to the seven competencies. The competencies, because they were derived directly from lead educators accomplishing great things under very challenging circumstances, provide a short but comprehensive agenda for leadership development. These skills combine the interactive power of push-and-pull forces. Challenging the status quo (competency one) and having a high sense of urgency for change and sustainable results (competency five) place non-negotiable priorities and performance front and center. Building trust through clear communication and expectations (competency two) and creating a commonly owned plan for success (competency three) develop clarity, specificity, and ownership relative to the agenda. Focusing on team over self (competency four) and committing to continuous improvement for self and organization (competency six) establish continuing learning for all as a requirement. Finally, focused involvement in building external networks and partnerships (competency seven) widens the arc of learning, engagement, and results.

The Seven Competencies

It is important to realize that no one is perfect and at the highest level on all of the seven competencies; the best leaders strive to improve on each one. You can begin your improvement process by completing Lyle's (Kirtman, 2014) self-assessment in his book. Another starting point is to determine what you believe are your strengths and areas for improvement on each competency and its traits. It would also be helpful to ask a trusted colleague, your supervisor, or your team for his or her assessment of you on each competency.

As you begin, use data from your last few evaluations to determine areas for improvement and connect them to the competencies. One popular practice is to complete a leadership inventory to determine areas for improvement. Lyle's (Kirtman, 2014) *Leadership and Teams: The Missing Piece of the Educational Reform Puzzle* reviews the research that directly connects the Workplace Personality Inventory to the seven competencies. This unique leadership research based on principal data provides sixteen specific areas to focus on, such as innovation, initiative, analyticity, achievement, and dependability. Each of the sixteen areas is tied to a specific competency.

Once you have determined the competencies that need improvement, the focus should only be on one or two. For example, let's look in detail at competency two—"builds trust through clear communication and expectations." You could take the following steps.

- Determine from any data—such as evaluations, 360 reviews, or self or team assessments—of your competencies what skill you need to develop. If you have difficulty being direct with people, that would be an important area to focus your improvement efforts. Match this area to the competency's traits (see figure 2.1, page 13). This area for improvement matches trait one—"is direct and honest about performance expectations."

- To improve this skill, it is important to explore why you have difficulty providing direct feedback. Is it because you do not like conflict or do not want to hurt relationships with people by being too direct? It could be that you are uncomfortable being in a leadership position and would rather just assume that people would do their jobs without you pointing out their areas for improvement.

- This self-exploration and analysis process is very important to determine the right strategies for you to pursue to change and improve. Perhaps you want to provide direct feedback but do not believe you know how to do it.

- A training program could be helpful on having crucial conversations or reading a book on critical feedback would work with your preferred way of learning.

- You would continue analyzing your data and connect them to each trait to begin your improvement effort. Trait two in competency two—"follows through with actions on all commitments"—is the second area. Training, reading, and self-exploration could be very helpful.

Is this hard work to really change and improve? Yes, but coping fruitlessly with the status quo is not that enjoyable either. It is easy to start the process, but the real work is sustaining your efforts and improvements over time. To create sustainable change, we recommend using a coach to help you through this process. The coach can be an objective person who can explore data with you and assist you in asking the right questions and looking at reality to determine high-leverage improvement strategies.

In the Napa Valley Unified School District, Patrick Sweeney, superintendent, is engaging his entire leadership cabinet on its individual and collective improvement on the seven competencies. Each cabinet member will determine two competencies for improvement. The cabinet will identify one competency for team improvement. The members will learn from each other and work on common improvement strategies. The cabinet will model the improvement process for the administrators throughout the district.

The principals and other administrators and managers will also be working on the seven competencies. Leadership and professional development and aspiring leaders programs will also be focusing on the seven competencies. The competencies will be tied to hiring practices for whole-system alignment. In fact, a goal for each person's performance evaluations will be tied to two of the seven competencies. All administrators support this systemwide process, which is shifting evaluation and performance improvements from the administrator out to his or her colleagues and supervisor instead of having the typical outside-in process or top-down efforts.

It's up to you.

These ideas are only meant to illustrate what it might look like to seriously delve into the seven competencies. The important thing is to have the big-picture issues that we addressed across the chapters as your template: you are not alone (chapter 1), move compliance aside (chapter 4), stay focused (chapter 5), make your organization a "come work with us" place to be (chapter 6), and realize that you can be successful anytime, anywhere (chapter 7) with these approaches that mobilize people for a great cause and make it possible for them to succeed.

We use the term *system player*. This is not an abstract term. It means that you operate in a fashion whereby you contribute to and benefit from the bigger picture. If you are a teacher, the slightly bigger picture may be your school as a whole. For a principal, it may mean other schools within the district. For all, it could mean other districts in your state or networks beyond your state and country.

New and potentially powerful forces are converging. It will take good leadership to take advantage of the possibilities—leaders who can model the seven competencies and can foster similar qualities in those they work with can make the difference. Move in these directions, and you will find many kindred spirits, and together you can overcome any obstacle that comes your way.

A new form of leadership is coming to the fore—we call it *leaders who lead*. Join the club! Make it a force for deep and systemic change. You are needed!

References & Resources

Accountability. (n.d.). In *Wikipedia*. Accessed at http://en.wikipedia.org/wiki/Accountability on December 31, 2014.

Anders, G. (2012, April 4). *Jeff Bezos's top 10 leadership lessons*. Accessed at www.forbes.com/sites/georgeanders/2012/04/04/bezos-tips/ on May 4, 2015.

Collins, J., & Porras, J. I. (2002). *Built to last: Successful habits of visionary companies*. New York: HarperCollins.

Covey, S. R. (1989). *The 7 habits of highly effective people: Restoring the character ethic*. New York: Simon & Schuster.

David, J. L., & Talbert, J. E. (2013). *Turning around a high-poverty district: Learning from Sanger*. San Francisco: S. H. Cowell Foundation.

DuFour, R., & Marzano, R. J. (2009). High-leverage strategies for principal leadership. *Educational Leadership, 66*(5), 62–68.

Fullan, M. (2010). *Motion leadership: The skinny on becoming change savvy*. Thousand Oaks, CA: Corwin Press.

Fullan, M. (2013). *Stratosphere: Integrating technology, pedagogy, and change knowledge*. Boston: Pearson.

Fullan, M. (2014). *The principal: Three keys for maximizing impact*. San Francisco: Jossey-Bass.

Fullan, M. (2015). *Freedom to change: Four strategies to put your inner drive into overdrive*. San Francisco: Jossey-Bass.

Fullan, M., & Quinn, J. (2015). *Coherence: The right drivers in action*. Thousand Oaks, CA: Corwin Press.

Goleman, D. (2013). *Focus: The hidden driver of excellence.* New York: HarperCollins.

Gordon Commission. (2013). *A public policy statement.* Princeton, NJ: Author.

Hargreaves, A., Boyle, A., & Harris, A. (2014). *Uplifting leadership: How organizations, teams, and communities raise performance.* San Francisco: Jossey-Bass.

Hargreaves, A., & Braun, H. (2012). *Leading for all: Final report to the Council of Directors of Education, Ontario.* Boston: Boston College.

Hargreaves, A., & Fullan, M. (2012). *Professional capital: Transforming teaching in every school.* New York: Teachers College Press.

Heath, D. (2004, July 15). *How to lead a switch.* Lecture presented at the GE Foundation Educators' Conference, Orlando, FL.

Heath, C., & Heath, D. (2010). *Switch: How to change things when change is hard.* New York: Broadway Books.

Jentz, B. C. (1982). *Entry.* New York: McGraw-Hill.

Jobs, S. (n.d.). *Quote on BrainyQuote.com.* Accessed at www.brainyquote .com/quotes/quotes/s/stevejobs416929.html on May 1, 2015.

Katzenbach, J. R., & Smith, D. K. (1993). The discipline of teams. *Harvard Business Review, 71*(2), 111–120.

Kirtman, L. (2014). *Leadership and teams: The missing piece of the educational reform puzzle.* Boston: Pearson.

Knudson, J. (2013). *You'll never be better than your teachers: The Garden Grove approach to human capital development.* Washington, DC: California Collaborative on District Reform.

Lencioni, P. (2012). *The advantage.* San Francisco: Jossey-Bass.

National Commission on Excellence in Education. (1983). *A nation at risk: The imperative for educational reform.* Washington, DC: U.S. Government Printing Office.

The Wallace Foundation. (2010). *Learning from leadership project: Investigating the links to improved student learning.* Accessed at www .wallacefoundation.org/knowledge-center/school-leadership/key -research/Documents/Investigating-the-Links-to-Improved-Student -Learning.pdf on June 15, 2015.

Waters, T., Marzano, R. J., & McNulty, B. (2003). *Balanced leadership: What 30 years of research tells us about the effect of leadership on student achievement.* Aurora, CO: Mid-continent Research for Education and Learning.

Index

A

accountability and compliance
  defined, 52
  effective use of time, 71–72
  finding time for, 60–62
  internal, 123–124
  micro-, 53
  new paradigm for, 56–59
  results-based culture, establishing a, 66–68
  self-management skills, building, 62–66
  shifting our focus on, 51–56
  tasks that matter, focusing on, 68–70
Advantage (Lencioni), 8
Amazon, 60, 101, 120
Ambrozavitch, S., 110–111
Antonucci, J., 103, 111
Apple, 60

B

Braun, H., 125
budget/financial issues, 114–117

C

California, leadership from the middle in, 126
Cambridge Innovation Center, 120
Cameron, A., 111

capacity building, 7, 24, 82
  See also leaders, capacity
central office service mentality, 82
change and results
  more than incremental, 119–121
  urgency for, 14, 27–30
coaching, 115–116
coherence, 81–82
Common Core State Standards (CCSS), 84, 124
communication, trust building and, 20
competencies. *See* seven leadership competencies
compliance. *See* accountability and compliance
continuous improvement, commitment to, 14, 30–32, 83
Covey, S., 63
creative insubordination, 69
Cullinane, C., 18–19

D

Dakin, P., 108
Darling-Hammond, L., 105
David, J., 84–85
Digital Equipment Corp., 119–120
DiSC, 12, 43, 103
drivers. *See* policy drivers
DuFour, R., 53

Cultures Built to Last
Richard DuFour, Michael Fullan
Take your professional learning community to the next level!
Discover a systemwide approach for re-envisioning your PLC while
sustaining growth and continuing momentum on your journey.
You'll move beyond pockets of excellence while allowing every
person to be an instrument of lasting cultural change.
BKF579

Change Wars
Edited by Andy Hargreaves and Michael Fullan
Michael Barber, Linda Darling-Hammond, Richard Elmore,
Michael Fullan, Andy Hargreaves, Jonathan Jansen, Ben Levin,
Pedro Noguera, Douglas Reeves, Andreas Schleicher,
Dennis Shirley, James Spillane, and Marc Tucker
What can organizations do to create profound, enduring changes?
International experts prove successful change can be a realistic
goal and then explore constructive alternatives to traditional
change strategies.
BKF254

The Collaborative Administrator
Austin Buffum, Cassandra Erkens, Charles Hinman,
Susan B. Huff, Lillie G. Jessie, Terri L. Martin, Mike Mattos,
Anthony Muhammad, Peter Noonan, Geri Parscale,
Eric Twadell, Jay Westover, and Kenneth C. Williams
In a culture of shared leadership, the administrator's role is
more important than ever. This book addresses your toughest
challenges with practical strategies and inspiring insight.
BKF256

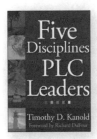

The Five Disciplines of PLC Leaders
Timothy D. Kanold
Foreword by Richard DuFour
Effective leadership in a professional learning community requires
practice, patience, and skill. Through engaging examples and
accessible language, this book offers a focused framework that
will help educators maintain balance and consistent vision as they
strengthen the skills of PLC leadership.
BKF495

Solution Tree | Press

a division of
Solution Tree

Visit solution-tree.com or call 800.733.6786 to order.

Wait! Your professional development journey doesn't have to end with the last pages of this book.

We realize improving student learning doesn't happen overnight. And your school or district shouldn't be left to puzzle out all the details of this process alone.

No matter where you are on the journey, we're committed to helping you get to the next stage.

Take advantage of everything from **custom workshops** to **keynote presentations** and **interactive web and video conferencing**. We can even help you develop an action plan tailored to fit your specific needs.

Let's get the conversation started.

Call 888.763.9045 today.

solution-tree.com